novum **premium**

MADAM RATTAN

Under the
RADAR

Snapshot of a
UK Dominatrix

novum 📖 premium

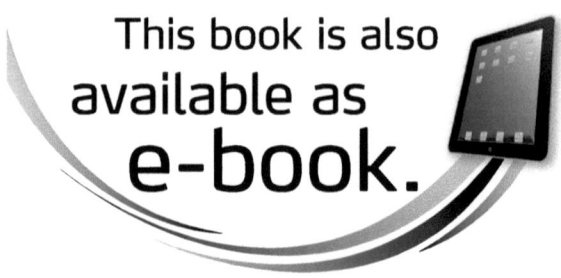

www.novum-publishing.co.uk

© 2022 novum publishing

ISBN 978-3-99130-130-1
Editing: Ashleigh Brassfield, DipEdit
Cover photos: Sergeybitos,
Starast | Dreamstime.com
Cover design, layout & typesetting:
novum publishing

www.novum-publishing.co.uk

Climate neutral
Print product
ClimatePartner.com/16547-2201-1002

Chapter One

Let's Wind Back the Clock;
A Monster Stops By; #MeToo;

The Start of the Adventure

It's quite hard to pinpoint exactly how things started. When I look back on growing up, I remember I always used to like watching television, and some of the things I saw on television really made a huge impact on me. I didn't realise it at the time, but I was subconsciously storing all sorts of information that I took on board in a big way. I always felt some of the images on television were intriguing, some extremely thought-provoking, and others very interesting. They definitely piqued more than my curiosity. They struck a chord – though at the time, I didn't know why!

We've all got a certain curiosity for different things. Some people are interested in haunted houses, while some even go to extremes, such as having an interest in murderers, zombies, martial arts, all sorts of things! Some people enjoy activities such as chess, quizzes, bingo, that type of thing; some like to push limits and get an adrenaline rush from mountain climbing, rock climbing, parachuting. Such a diverse cross-section of different things; but my curiosity, my interests, often seemed to involve things of a sexual nature.

When I was around twelve or thirteen years old, I remember seeing a Dominatrix torturing somebody. I think she had him on a step ladder. Anyway, I saw she'd hooked up this pulley system contraption and had his genitals tied up to this rope/braid pulley system, while tugging at these weights in a bucket. I can't remember much else about it, but that scene just stuck in my head and stayed with me. I'd love to know which programme it was. There were other programmes where I used to watch people doing 'naughty' things to other people, which also held my attention.

I always watched TV programmes that had an interest or element about the sex industry. I found them really fascinating – I couldn't peel my eyes off the screen. There was one series in the nineties I particularly remember called 'The Vice'. Every episode was filled with various themes of sex-related escapades and predicaments that really opened up my thirst for knowledge about alternative sexualities. I absorbed it all.

In those days, as I remember most, if not all, programmes were about male/female, never about male/male or female/female. How things have changed; thank goodness. People are more open minded, less misogynistic – a politician might say, "the direction of travel is going the right way." And it certainly is. About time.

My parents were amazing, but poor. They were very hardworking, never smoked or drank, and saved their money to buy bricks and mortar. They were from an era where that was the most important goal to them; both from poor families, the pressure to succeed with the material possession of a house, their castle, was great – that and bringing their children up to have freedom of choice without pressure and to believe they could do whatever they believed they could do.

I loved horses. It all started when we used to drive through the New Forest when we drove down to Bournemouth to see my grandparents; the New Forest is one of the UK's national parks and is full of wild horses, which are owned by the commoners, who have automatic grazing rights. I loved it. It fuelled my dreams and fantasies on the long, boring car journeys.

It's an expensive hobby.

Was that going to stop me? No! With luck, determination and ingenuity I bagged a volunteer job at the local riding stables in exchange for rides – lots of rides. I was so hardworking I was even allowed to give others lessons; I was a lovely child and got on so well with just about everyone.

I was even allowed to take a pony to a horse show that was being held locally and sat next to Princess Anne and chatted to her. I had lessons from the daughter of the owner, who was really mean to me and made me have all my lessons bareback, which was extremely hard but so good for my riding technique.

My dad used to transport me and a car full of helpers to and from the stables; my parents were just pleased I wasn't bored and playing out on the street. In the then-freezing winters my feet would be frozen from morning till I got home; one Saturday a horse trod on my toe and I didn't realise it was damaged 'til I got home, took my boot off and found my damaged and bloody toe! And I loved every minute, I was so innocent. So naïve. So young and so not streetwise.

And then the stables closed down. We were bereft.

I wasn't about to let that stop my passion for horses, so my mum and I devised a plan. My father had opened up a bank account for myself and my brother; he ran it and called it 'instant banking'. He paid interest, and I divided my pocket money into all sorts of different projects; presents, horse, holidays, etc. It really encouraged me with the power of saving for something bigger (I am sure that's why I am good with figures & bookkeeping).

We saved up (pocket money and housekeeping savings). To help boost our savings we went to the supermarket at the end of the day and bought the marked down purchases; Christmas was best, the shops shut for a few days then and all fresh food had to go, and it went cheap. My dad went round the back of the fruit and veg market stalls, not the fronts, and did deals on boxes of damaged fruit. We ate like kings, sometimes.

Savings, well, we were good at that.

And so, in time we had saved about £50 and we went to Reading Horse Sales (my favourite place every month; 50 horses and 700 lots of saddlery, I was in heaven) and bought my little pony. Several moves of stables to keep him in ensued and after much determined study of the locality, I managed to find an unused, huge field which was a few hundred metres from my house! It was the most beautiful pasture, old oak trees, little copses and spinneys, and alongside the local golf course. Bliss: I managed to find a few young lasses who owned ponies and we shared the cost of the rental. We were in heaven.

After a short time there, a disagreeable neighbour found a loophole in the lease; it stated the field was only to be used for livestock, or some such rubbish. We were all evicted at the end of the month. My dream came crashing down, so once again the sheer determination kicked in and the search for a new home for my pony started once more.

I managed to find a stable and small paddock on Mr Podberry's chicken farm, a few miles away, a bike ride. A lovely old farmer, he had retired but still wanted to remain active and kept chickens. There were hundreds of them, and they loved him and followed him everywhere; he would reach into his brown warehouse coat pocket and sprinkle some chicken feed around for his girls! What a character. I was very lucky to find this facility.

The other girls found a small farm on the main A4 and they moved there.

Of course, we all kept in touch. If I hadn't been so friendly with them, I often wonder how my life would have gone.

How significant that desire to maintain friendships was.

I was at the most significant junction of my life and had no idea.

The owner of the farm was a young man called Hans. He was charming and fun, and encouraged the girls to play in the straw and have potato fights in the field; he joined in, of course, and when I visited, so did I.

Slowly a relationship formed. He was 24 and I was 10 years younger, 14 years old. In those days, it wasn't thought of as strange. My parents were poor, and his parents were rich; he dangled riches before me, and I felt unable to refuse.

My parents felt awful they could not provide the means to further my hobby, but they supported me in whatever way they could. They came and helped on the farm and with the ponies there. I was a good rider, good at showjumping; not the best, but I had promise.

He could provide the very thing I had craved, access to a lifestyle I had dreamed about, and that was exactly what he did. He was flashy, with his Lotus sports car and brand new Range Rover. His parents were so rich, their house in Jersey on the seafront, that they would send their Rolls Royce to pick me up from the airport – me, flying! It was unheard of unless you were from a privileged class. The farm they bought him in Henley-on-Thames when the land on the A4 was sold for building had neighbours like Lord Heseltine and record producers; even George Harrison lived down the road. The possibilities for my future and the temptations were too great for an impressionable and ambitious young girl.

I had spent my younger years dreaming about owning a stable full of horses, planning and drawing the layout of the stable yard, pretending to buy the saddlery, circling adverts of horses for sale in the magazine Horse & Hound, even naming them! Scouring pages of adverts for wooden stables, sheds, showjumps, horse boxes; you name it, I had dreamed it and planned it.

To have someone who tempted me with the fulfilment of that dream, that fantasy; for a young and naïve, unworldly girl, that temptation was impossible to refuse. He took me leaps and bounds closer to achieving my dream, I had all the ideas, he had the cold hard cash – or rather his parents did, and they kept on drip-feeding it to him, bit by bit, and he drew me in, bit by bit.

And yes, then there was the sex. Of course, he held off for a while – when I met him I was only 14 – but once I was on the pill, the situation developed. He had regular sex with me when he wanted; I thought I was being really grown up and clever, being the first girl in my class to have a 'proper' boyfriend. Sex education at home and school was non-existent. I had bagged a rich and generous man, and I was way under 16. How easily it happened, and I concealed the sexual part from my parents. I didn't know much about sex, but did I know deep down that it was wrong?

Lots of kids have sex underage, of course. Had it been just the relationship with sex, well I wouldn't be writing this and my journey in life would have been very different. But he took pictures – he developed his own pictures, he had a special room and we always went there to take the pictures. Until recently I never thought anything about this.

And I thought I was so clever.

In the very early 1970's He took me to seedy Soho sex shops and bought me outfits. He loved taking pictures of me in my school uniform, in mini skirt poses while I walked up the stairs, meanwhile drawing me in further and further by dangling the means to a future I had dreamed of.

Still, I thought I was so clever.

When I think back, I also remember that he used to drive past me most days when I was walking to school along the A4; in my naïveté I thought it was fate that had brought us together. Was it?

Did I subconsciously realise this was wrong? Not sure. I thought I was living an exciting life; missing school a lot, my schoolwork suffered, my attitude changed. I was enjoying a life I could not have had under normal circumstances, so if I had doubts, I buried them and continued living a life of which my family had no idea.

A double life, a secret life, an exciting life, a seedy life; a life that was to be buried in my mind for 40-plus years and only surface due to two specific things that happened.

The main reason is the lockdown. It gave me time to slow my mind, to sit and think, to process the past, something I had steadfastly refused to do apart from the occasional flashback.

The other trigger was an account of a shocking act from an abuse survivor who was reaching out to me. Rushing to my thoughts came details I had buried but not forgotten.

For all these years I have been quite a workaholic, burying myself in either work or study. I had either worked a 60-hour week or had two jobs, or had a job and studied hard for formal exams to make up for the way I missed school while under the influence/spell of Hans and his riches and sordidness.

I did all this while being a single parent family for much of the time, with two children and two marriages. I made some truly awful choices in men.

When I had problems with people I would either cut them off completely, or get stuck in a superficial groove, going over and around the issue again and again like a stuck record, keeping myself busy and getting hung up on my day to day problems. I avoided delving into my formative years; maybe it was just too painful. Our minds have a way of protecting us. Maybe I just wasn't ready or didn't want to deal with the consequences of what had happened.

The consequences were mental, not physical. Mental scars can be buried forever, or they can be dwelled on daily, enough to prevent people from moving forward.

Or, like me, they can be buried and come back to haunt you at a later date; for me it was when my mind stopped working overtime. It all started to come together and make sense when it was stilled and rested.

I began to feel able to talk more freely about it. *Because while I didn't tell anyone, well, it hadn't really happened, had it?*

Of course, I had never forgotten about this (I had even referred to it a couple of times in the last 10 years); I had refused to be a victim and refused to let it destroy my life, as it can so easily do, though of course it had shaped my life, even though I refused to admit it.

I found a coping strategy that worked well for me: keeping busy and refusing to become a victim that was stuck in a rut of memories, unable to break out. We have all seen that happen, people spending so much time looking back that they fail to see the life they could be enjoying.

But I do think, in some strange way, it eventually allowed me to be open minded about anything to do with sex. How? I don't know. Maybe because this happening in my formative years, well, I thought taking provocative pictures was the norm; it didn't occur to me that I was a child of course.

Sex was something adults did, and as a teenager, I probably liked to think I knew it all. I do know that I was troublesome at school; I made some teachers lives unbearable, being unruly, cheeky, and missing a lot of school. My exams suffered and I left grammar school with a meagre O level and a CSE.

Was the journey I eventually took in the world of Female Domination a way of letting go of my anger, though I never felt angry?

Hans taught me a lot about business; his parents had made lots and lots of money, so much they became residents of Jersey. I looked after his farm accounts and did his VAT.

It became apparent he wasn't as nice as I thought he was; he was cruel to animals. The RSPCA visited him regularly and they even took him to court for cruelty to pigs, and, if my memory serves me correctly, he was banned for life for keeping pigs. He didn't feed them. He was a *horrible* man, and feeding his animals, well, that often became my job.

When his parents bought him the farm at Henley-on-Thames, he bought lots of very young calves to fatten for beef. Calves need a lot of milk to grow, but he kept them in a big shed with no water. I had to carry the water every day in five-gallon containers, filled from a standpipe. When he used to go and visit his parents in Jersey, he never left enough food for the animals. One visit, I had to bag up a ton of barley (harvested from his fields) into 1cwt sacks, load them on a tractor and trailer, and take them to the corn and seed merchants to put a credit on the account so I could buy feed. I was strong and very fit then, plus I was very determined.

Later on in our relationship I also had a part-time job in a bank.

Another Jersey trip I managed to get a bank loan of around £500 in order to buy the animals their food; he never paid me back, of course. It was a constant battle to feed the animals he insisted on buying. And yet he kept buying me things; he bought me an ex-hurdler from the famous trainer Captain Tim Foster. I loved that horse. When we split, he took him away and shut him up in a stable.

So much happened that I now look back on and wonder about.

I got a job at a bank that he banked with, as he knew the bank manager. *I didn't even have an interview,* his influence with the bank made for a job offer for me. I was 16 and had left school with minimal qualifications. My mind had been elsewhere. The first day I started work the manager wasn't there; the rumour was that he had been sacked for having smutty magazines in his office. Who knows? Just how did Hans wangle me a job?

At Hans' house, why were the photos always taken in the same room?

I remember one evening we went round to someone's house, I can't remember what for; to be friends, I think. I remember that the man was a policeman. Why was he friends with a policeman that he had never mentioned?

I didn't make sense of all these seemingly insignificant actions until other high-profile cases came to light. I was a naïve child who thought she was a woman who had control and was getting what she dreamed of; was I the one being manipulated and used? Or was this just a catalogue of unrelated and innocent coincidences?

Driving by me on my walk to school;
The bank manager who liked smutty pictures;
The policeman;
The trips to Soho for sexy outfits;
The photographs developed himself;
The one room that was always used.

They could be coincidences, but do the photographs and the room make them something far more sinister altogether?

You decide.

I do think that he loved me, but his personality was so dark (and spoiled) that I started to resent the way he treated animals and people; I started to argue back, he started to become physically violent.

After the second incident of physical violence, I decided to quit the relationship.

Then followed one of the most emotionally difficult times in my life. He tried to get me to come back to him.

13

He was angry, threatening to take back every single present he had ever bought me.

He was distraught, begging me to come back.

He even resorted to threatening his own wellbeing.

He promised me the world, said we would get married.

His mum bought him a red Ferrari, a supercar; she did what she always did when her son was upset, spend money on him to soothe his feelings. Did it work? For a little while, maybe. He even insured it for me to drive it and attempted to blackmail me into coming back.

He was still distraught. He would turn up at my house in the evenings begging, crying, shouting, screaming for me to go back. This lasted weeks; it was really hard to stand and watch a grown man cry and beg like that.

The easiest thing would have been to go back, for so many different reasons. But it was too late. When he eventually realised I wasn't coming back, he turned nasty, as he often did when he didn't get his own way, and took back every single thing he had bought me, as he had previously threatened.

I didn't care. I was free of the toxicity of that relationship. Had I stayed, I would have been a possession, that's all. In a gilded cage, yes, but a possession nonetheless. I learned a lesson that I will never forget: *money cannot buy you happiness*, and money doesn't always buy you what you want – sometimes it just buys you a load of trouble. Yes, I know it's an old cliché, but I can say it with experience of what money can do to people.

Nowadays, the lasting legacy is that I still cannot cope with emotional pressure of people constantly asking for something; I just cave in. I vowed not to get involved with anyone who was emotionally manipulative. I tried anyway.

So, I did all the things we all do; settled down, married (twice), had children, had jobs, was self-employed, moved around. When I needed stability for my children because I was a single parent, in the 1990's I joined the Civil Service and eventually moved north on promotion and stayed there until my children had both gone to university.

My exploration into an alternative lifestyle started in the last couple of years that I was still in the CS. My son, a very sensitive young man, concluded I was a free spirit and told me to leave the CS and be free, and so I did.

I feel sure that this bad relationship affected and moulded my feelings towards the alternative lifestyle.

Time moves on, and when I reflect I remember one of my husband's friends saying to me, "Why do you always talk to me like you are a school teacher?"

"Do I?" We had a great friendship, he made me laugh a lot and he used to like helping us with decorating the house when I was around. This was the writing on the wall and I still had no idea!

Fast forward and I don't know exactly how my journey into BDSM became a reality. I guess the nearest I can think of is when online chatrooms were still allowed, and you could write something about yourself online. You could click onto other people's profiles and find out all about them. I used to love doing that. I find people really fascinating and, on this particular site, you could find out all about their sexual interests. It was so diverse ... and I was excited & interested by the whole thing.

One guy's profile in particular really stood out for me. I remember it really well. He was gay and he'd explored his sexuality with men, as a male companion. He described it in great detail; all about his travels all around the world and what an amazing time he'd had! He made it sound so fantastic, and it caught my imagination! *I want to do that! I want to travel the world and stay in fantastic hotels! Exotic travels, exotic lifestyle, interwoven with sex! Yes! That's for me!* I was sure of it.

I loved to travel, and I loved to stay in quality hotels. Another seed was sown. I remember at the bottom of his profile there was a link to a site called *'Alt.com'*. It was a sex site covering all sorts of genres. It intrigued me so much, I joined the site right there and then!

It wasn't a dating site. It was a site where you promoted yourself. So, while setting up my profile, I figured, *Well, I've got lovely breasts*, as I sized them up, *let's focus on these. My breasts have always been my best asset, I've always hidden them away, so let's celebrate them!* So I focused on my breasts and then, lo and behold, people were writing to me! Loads of them! It was bizarre! It was fun! It was enlightening! So many people were interested ... in me! It gave me a renewed sense of confidence. It left me on a high.

It was on this old '.com' site where I met this guy from London. We struck up a chord and started having regular online chats. He said he could never come up and see me because he lived with his wife. They were both retired.

"That's okay," I said to him, "perhaps we can just chat?" I gleaned a lot of information from him. It gave me an incredible insight of a completely different lifestyle. He was submissive and interested in submission. He was the one who gave me a new and different perspective that soon took on a whole new life of its own.

I also met up with other people who I'll mention later on in the book. There was Terry from Manchester; Steve from the north; and Peter. Everyone I was in contact with was always male. I wasn't interested, nor was I looking, for females at that time.

Peter, who I've just mentioned, was trying to "dip his toe in the water." I remember he'd always said he had feelings that he wanted to submit to a powerful lady. He wanted to try it out but was scared. His fetish was for high heels; it had begun when he was a child of six or seven. One day, he told me, he'd come home from school and brought a friend with him. They were playing with their Dinky toys on the wood parquet flooring in the dining room when his friend's mother came to pick his friend up. He remembered he could hear her 'tip-tapping' across the floor in her high heels, then picking Peter up by his ear, saying sternly, "And what do you think you're doing!" Well! That, he said, was enough to set his mind wanting for a long, long time. That was his pivotal, defining moment.

I should mention that all names have been changed unless they are an alias/alter-ego's name – I have permission to use alter ego names.

I made friends online with a lot of people, including 'bbc-boy', who was a huge caning enthusiast and would travel the world to get his 'fix'. He just loved to be caned! He was the one who taught me how to cane. He was so patient. He lived in Scotland and used to come down to my base in the north after having picked fresh birch and made a 'birch' for me to cane him with. How considerate! We had a spanking bench in the dungeon, and he just bent over that bench and let me practice and practice and practice … it was glorious! And so was his backside by the time I'd finished!

In the beginning, when I was practicing my caning skills, I used a feather pillow to hone my technique, covering it in talc so I could see where the strokes were. I became quite adept and was able to cane quite accurately, partly because of practice and partly, I think, because I used to ride horses. I was familiar with wielding a whip, you see. Not that I used to go around whipping the horses! I was just used to how it felt and knew about the different weights and things.

'bbc-boy' used to let me practice on him to my heart's content – and his heart's content! He loved it. We had fun in all kinds of ways, like the positions in which he'd stand. If I stood too close, he'd get 'wrap-around', which means that when the cane hits, it flicks to the soft part of the outer thigh and marks very easily. It didn't matter really, but it all helped make me accurate at caning.

He remained a friend for a good number of years. We had all sorts of escapades and experiences together. He was a hard-core masochist. He was along the same level of masochism as Justin Stripes, who I'll introduce a little later in another chapter. Yes, bbc-boy was definitely hard-core. He travelled the world for it. He went to Thailand regularly to visit Mistresses he had read about or seen caning online. He went all over. That's how serious he wanted it, needed it, in his life.

I used to meet and talk with lots and lots of submissives. When I was meeting submissives for the first time, we would often meet at a coffee shop in the train station. I always arranged to meet in a very public place. I used to tell them to stand underneath the clock and look them over, checking them out from a distance. If I felt uncomfortable in any way, I could turn away. I am always thorough in my research; so much so, that in every rendezvous I arranged with a potential sub, I did always end up meeting them face-to-face. Never once did I feel uncomfortable.

On the initial meeting I would chat to them for about an hour. We'd have a really good chat, just so I could find out all about them. For me, it was all down to chemistry. I had to have that feeling; the feeling that I could talk to them, and they could talk to me – that they were open and honest. If they didn't have that certain something, then I didn't pursue it. I used to tell people most of the time, there and then, "You know, it's been lovely having a chat with you but I just don't think we're compatible enough," looking them straight in the eye, "sorry, but we haven't got the same interests." I would finish it there and then, and that would be it.

There were lots of people I continued to stay friends with over the years, including a sub I met who lived in Carlisle. He had MS. I spent a lot of time going to see him. He bought me the most lovely gifts, he really did. When I used to drive to Carlisle, he used to make me afternoon tea, get me my favourite biscuits out and wait on me hand and foot. He used to like to dress up as a maid; that's what gave him his enjoyment. He bought me some beautiful, beautiful whips. A lovely person. I kept in contact with him for many years.

All these different people that I had relationships with, they taught me a lot about the way people tick, what they think and what they do; how things start; how things lie dormant in people and why people want to do different things. Everyone has their own fascinating story to tell.

It's like a jigsaw. When you find that missing piece, suddenly the whole jigsaw makes sense. For me, I think some of the biggest pieces that made up my jigsaw were all the films I used to watch – and all the documentaries too! They just fuelled my imagination. And, of course, my experiences in my teenage years gave me a whole, entirely new and completely different perspective of alternative preferences.

All these things that happened in my life, yet I still can't put my finger on what the trigger was that joined all the pieces together and started me on my journey. Was it my teenage years, when I was so impressionable? They call it a journey. It is a journey, because it's a journey of exploration to find out about yourself; about myself; to dig deep; to see what makes you tick; to be honest with yourself. And it was time for me to be honest with myself.

Being a Mistress ticked many boxes for me. In my opinion, it's all about indulgence on a long-term scale. It's never about a 'quick fix', or to make a 'quick buck'! It has to be with the right person. That's why the chemistry has to be right. For me, it has to be a win-win situation. But for many Dommes it just doesn't matter. There are those who believe it doesn't matter that it doesn't matter; I can only surmise they may simply believe they are fulfilling other people's long held fantasies rather than their own.

But I can't speak for others, I can only speak for myself. I am not necessarily right, it's just what worked for me. I think that the role playing involved in this lifestyle/game/scene enabled me to somewhat balance what had happened to me as a teenager; I hadn't managed to control that situation very well, but I was damn sure I would control this part of the journey, I think my bossiness had been building over the years until it culminated at this juncture in life that I found myself at, *but* it had to be win-win. I didn't want to entertain any sort of relationship where it was win-lose, so the consensual part of this was paramount. Would I get pleasure from caning someone who didn't want to be caned? Absolutely not!

I remember one of my old Civil Service bosses giving me feedback when I hadn't got a promotion I was well qualified for. He told me I was certainly capable, but I never sold myself fully. He suggested I take up Amateur Dramatics. It would be a way to express myself; a good way to practice confidence boosting ideas. *What?!* Little did he know I had plans of my own!

In my mind, being a Mistress was a perfect way for me to explore areas I was unable to explore in a vanilla relationship; and just because I had relationships with all these different people didn't necessarily mean I had to have sex with them either! I like that arrangement. It suited me perfectly. One of the things I like about the BDSM scene and its community is that they are always so completely non-judgemental. So refreshing! So liberating! So freeing!

Unfortunately, a lot of people aren't always honest with themselves ... at all! They kid themselves about things. But being a submissive? It peels back all the layers. They're down on their knees in front of someone, a Mistress or a Master, to be whipped ... or perhaps their nipples played with ... or whispered in their ear. It takes a certain humility to be able to do that.

It's always had me wondering, *how on earth do these people know that they are submissive? Or that they wanted pain? How did they find out?* I think it's quite amazing. A lot of people go through life not being happy and not knowing *why* they're not happy. I usually do try and find out what leads people to this alternative lifestyle; the stories are fascinating, and most of them are all slightly different! Though caning enthusiasts often have a shared theme, as you will find out later.

I've discovered from submissives that there are a number of elements that give them a deep, deep need. A stressful workload, responsibility, childhood, lasting impressions, trauma ... all manner of life experiences that build into the very fabric of their being which, if they are being honest, need to be assuaged, eased, released, attended to, nurtured ... recognised ... seen ... heard ... understood ...

It's an innate thing. Something that doesn't go away. Something that's always there and flares up when they least expect it. And to deny it? A grave mistake that haunts them. It never goes away. It can be diminished and 'put in the shadows', but it never disappears completely.

Being authentic, honest, and acknowledging these tendencies is a freeing and liberating experience to some submissives; it makes them soar, go places they could never go otherwise! It's difficult to understand that to be tied up, whipped, flogged, caned, whatever their preference, can be the means to set them free.

I remember Albert, a very high-ranking official in the Defence industry. He used to travel the world, working for a very large organisation with a huge responsibility for contracts and, ultimately, people's jobs. A very large, ruthless organisation. He was a dapper gentleman of a certain age who was very proper, very proper indeed. He was used to talking to Government officials at all levels … and he wanted to submit to a powerful, strong Mistress. He just wanted to be bossed around. He wanted to balance his life.

And what an interesting man! He would drive up to see me and take me out for dinner. I remember I was totally mesmerised at the fact that he was wearing a Rolex watch. I've always had dreams of being able to afford a Rolex. And there he was, as casually as you please, wearing one.

I remained friends with him for a long, long time. Often he would come up around Christmas and New Year, stay at an upmarket hotel overlooking the river and invite me out to dinner. Many, many a time he asked me to marry him. It was the same old thing. He wanted to settle down with a strong woman.

Once he booked me on a long-haul flight to fly out and meet him where he was working. He'd actually booked me a First Class seat on the plane. Not only was it First Class, he'd booked seat number one! He sent me the tickets for it! He wasn't just talking, he actually did it! I was gob-smacked!

Unfortunately, I never got to go. I'd been looking forward to it for ages, then about two weeks before, there was unrest in the country and the Foreign Office advised people not to travel. I had to cancel! *No!* I was gutted! That was a good few years ago now, though, but so bizarre. I remember it as if it were yesterday.

The thrill of being able to do the things that were way beyond my parents reach, that they loved to do, and the times we had such good adventures; the pull of being able to do those things as an adult was impossible for me to reject.

That was the start of my adventure. I haven't mentioned everybody that I've met yet, just a few people, but the one I had the greatest interaction with was Steve. You will read about him in another chapter.

Chapter Two

London; Sugar Daddy Beginnings

Today I'm embarking on my journey, I thought excitedly. Most encounters I'd had so far had been via online fetish sites. It was all about making friends and building up a network of fetishists with people on the scene who embrace the lifestyle which was to become my trademark.

One of those friends included a male submissive who was older than me, lived in London and was happily married. It was convenient for both of us to have this online arrangement because it fitted in nicely with our schedules and we were happy with that. Over time, we built up a strong online friendship.

As I said, he was getting older, was happily married, retired, and because he spent most of his time with his wife, meeting online was the only option … he just couldn't get away from his wife!

He also couldn't get away from the deep feelings he had of being submissive. Over the time I got to know him, I realised it wasn't an ideal scenario for him; It was more like a 'halfway house' having this online friendship. Still, he was happy to impart his knowledge and feelings about being a submissive to a Mistress embarking on her journey of discovery.

We stayed in contact for months, until one day, totally out of the blue, he messaged me, "I have the most amazing opportunity for us to spend some time together. My wife's going to America for a few days. Why don't you come down to visit me while she's away?"

He wanted me to fly down to London and stay at his home! For two nights! *What!* Of course, I refused. I'd never even met the guy! After some discussion, however, we finally reached a compromise, and I flew down early one Sunday morning. We arranged for him to meet me at the airport.

I spotted him as soon as I walked through the double doors. Being an internal flight, he was sitting there waiting for me in the little room. His eyes, scouring the people as they walked through the double doors, recognised me immediately. He stood up to greet me but was suddenly stopped short when somebody came up to him who he obviously knew and started chatting to him ...

"Fancy seeing you here ..." It was one of his neighbours! He took it all in his stride. *Very professional,* I observed. With his posh accent and relaxed demeanour, I realised he was used to handling difficult situations. He certainly didn't appear fazed by it. He was, by all accounts, quite a powerful man. Apparently, he used to manage a huge farm in South America.

Once the pleasantries were over, he escorted me to his car, stowed my bags, then drove me back to his apartment. The roads were busy and detours were everywhere. We had gotten caught up among the leaders and pacers of the London Marathon. The elite had already crossed the finish line, and amateur club runners with the fastest times were already proudly displaying their medals. *What a day!* I thought. *What more could happen? How on earth is this all going to end up?!*

Eventually we arrived at his apartment. It was the most beautiful Victorian block of apartments I'd ever seen, and it was overlooking the Thames! *Wow!* I mused, *clearly managing a farm abroad all these years has paid well.* It was obvious when he showed me round the spacious rooms with tasteful décor and works of art, all carefully and strategically placed. He was a man of substance, and his wealth of abundance was visually quite substantial.

He wasted no time in letting me know what he wanted ... he'd bought me an E-Stim machine! A machine that sends mild to strong – to very strong – impulses through the skin to stimulate muscles and nerves. I practised using the electro-stimulator on him to my heart's content, seeing how the levels of pain instilled different reactions, from sighs of ecstasy to screams of pure torture, throughout the entire London Marathon. The roar of the crowds, the applause, and the continuous running commentary booming out from the PA speakers across London were a wonderful backdrop to the writhing mass that was on the floor at my feet ... and he loved it! It became quite apparent that he was not a submissive, he was a masochist, masked as a submissive to get the very thing he craved.

I didn't need to stay for the two days. He was more than satisfied with a day writhing on the floor as I gained confidence! I started to realise the power I was developing. He drove me back to the airport and I was on the evening flight home that very night. *What a day!* I thought for the second time that day as I stopped flicking through the pages of the flight magazine to take a delightful sip of the miniature Prosecco the stewardess had kindly given me. *And this is just the beginning! Wow!* I reflected in amazement. *Okay, that's it! I'm hooked!* This was so exciting! I'd fallen in love with the lifestyle. I love flying, travelling, going places, and my confidence was increasing every day ... *Ah yes, this is definitely the life for me!* I vowed as I nestled more comfortably in my seat.

When I received his message to say how much he loved our spontaneous meet I was thrilled! He loved it so much he wanted more. He was prepared to pay all my expenses for the privilege ... and he kept his word. He paid for me to come down to London every five to six weeks, would put me up in a hotel for three nights, and, because he could only visit me a couple of times for a couple of hours in the afternoons due to his restricted schedule, I was mostly free to entertain myself in London. All expenses paid! I had landed on my feet.

But I was bored.

From his extensive teachings and my keenness to learn, I discovered more and more about the mindset of a submissive and masochist. Armed with this knowledge and free to roam London, I started doing sessions and began to build and expand my own 'stable' ... gathering my own submissives 'at my pleasure'.

Whatever I made in London was all mine, because he paid for my hotel, travel and dinner for three nights ... and it wasn't cheap! This arrangement lasted a couple of years, until he got too old and retired gracefully. And every time I visited London, I stayed at the Hilton Hotels.

When the time came for me to pay my own way, Hilton Hotels were doing a special offer in conjunction with my new credit card, saying, "Stay three times and get a free night's stay." I needed to spend so much money in three months to collect points on the VIP card, which would eventually qualify me for Silver status.

From then on, staying at the Hilton was something I never changed. I very rarely stayed in any other type of hotel. I built up my status and became a Platinum card holder ... free breakfast with a room upgrade! By this time, I was paying for the room myself. This offer upgraded me to the Executive Suite of the hotel, with its own private lounge, rooms, and patio area.

Luxury hotels were the most popular choice because they didn't ask too many questions. Having a woman staying at the hotel and a man checking in to 'visit' was an unusual assumption which people didn't easily make. Generally, it's the other way round ... I feel sure this is due to the psychological and cultural phenomenon of women not being equal to men, that it was never assumed a man was being dominated by a woman or whatever.

When I initially started travelling, there weren't many of us doing it. Most just stayed in their locality. A few *did* travel, but there weren't many. An online website called *'Eros'* used to have a travelling section. You could advertise yourself at a new temporary location for a reasonable fee; though it was mainly used by escorts, it did have visiting dominatrix adverts as well.

In London there's a lot of Mistresses, a lot of them fly-by-nights wanting to make a quick buck for little effort. There's a lot of competition. A lot of men are addicted to the thrill of meeting somebody new ... ... new and potentially dangerous. These Mistresses are young, beautiful model-types. They never appeared to be having as good a time as I was over the years, as they never stayed around for long. Then again, they never did what I did. They weren't of the same mindset. It was always about something else that they wanted for themselves ... and a plethora of bitchiness to boot!

I gleaned a lot of satisfaction in the fact I defied all the stereotypes that people imagined of Mistresses; I was short, round, and over fifty. And I'll tell you what ... I did alright.

The people who contacted me were more in tune with their inner self. They were not doing anything 'on a whim'. No. These were the type who prioritised their wants and needs carefully and utilised their emotional intelligence to the degree of wanting me and my particular 'brand' of what I offered, as opposed to a sexually charged image of what they *thought* they wanted.

My particular brand with BDSM was caning. I'm also bossy. To some people, that was enough.

Being organised and bossy can be very attractive to some people, so I did fine. I met some very interesting people along the way and have been to some fantastic places, all paid for. I used to like that, because it defied the general consensus society upholds of what you have to do, or be, to be successful. I didn't have to prove anything to anybody. I was good at what I did. I excelled at caning. Being successful, to me, has never been about money and earning so much of it; my past life taught me that money can buy you things but may not make you happy. Living life, making people happy, and having unusual and exciting experiences was far more potent to me.

Arriving in the capital after the train journey to Euston, I would always take a black Hackney cab from the station to the hotel in Kensington. I loved those half hour jaunts. I loved talking to the drivers. I'd always get to find out all about what's going on with the people and places I was visiting. Different cultures fascinate me, and taxi drivers are definitely a diverse culture. They're usually happy, friendly, and chatty. Great characters from all walks of life.

On one such visit, I'm chatting away to the taxi driver about his life. I'm explaining I'm working in London when he points to the canvas pool cue bag I carry my canes in.

"What's that then?" he asked in a friendly, amicable tone.

"Oh, it's a fishing rod." I tried to sound nonchalant. "I'm just delivering it to somebody," I answered. Discretion is the most important thing. He was such a nice taxi driver … When he dropped me off, I followed my instincts: "By the way," I said, tongue-in-cheek, "it isn't a fishing rod in there. It's my canes. I'm in London to cane people!" I proclaimed, expecting to shock him. Instead, he surprised me.

"Thought you were. Magic! That's lovely, that."

I really got the impression he was interested enough to ask for my phone number. He probably would've done if I'd told him in the cab earlier, not while I was getting out of the car. *A missed opportunity there, ah well,* I thought as I swept through the double doors and into the hotel foyer to check-in.

Chapter Three

London; Justin Stripes;
Stolen Bag; Purple Palace

Justin Stripes is a legend on the fetish scene who just loves to be caned! I had tried to arrange a meeting with Stripes on my trips to London several times, but had failed dismally. In the end I just gave up. He was never available, always jetting off to some country or another through his day job.

I gave him one final try when he eventually said we could meet next time I was in London. We arranged to meet at the foyer of the Hotel at Kensington. This time we did!

We had afternoon tea in a quiet corner, out of the way of prying ears … our conversation was not for the faint-hearted. It was for our benefit only. So, we chatted. After finishing our in-depth discussion, I reached for my bag on the floor which I'd placed to my left, nestled between me and a large, structured pillar, just to the left of the sofa. And it wasn't there! My bag had gone!

What! Where is it! It can't have just walked! It can't be! It can't be gone! I felt panic rising up in my chest. I got to my feet and slowly walked round the perimeter of the pillar. *It must be here! It must be!*

I looked up, my eyes boring directly into Stripes' in total shock. "It's gone! Stripes! My bag! It's gone!" I was frantic. "It was right here!" I shrieked, pointing to the floor, "Right here! Right next to me! Stripes! My lovely bag!" I wailed. "With all of my stuff! It's gone! I've been here all the time! Where. Is. My. Bag?! Stripes!"

I was absolutely gutted! Everything of any value for my London trip was in it. My beautiful, soft, red leather Prada handbag! It was medium-sized, yet deceptively large inside … it was beautiful. My favourite! Gone!

It had my phone, my money, my train ticket home ... very expensive make up. I only buy quality make up. It was worth hundreds!

I wracked my brain. *Agh! My USB stick! With all my fetish photos on! Shit! My purse ... my credit cards ...* I howled in anguish. I was devastated!

I scoured the ground floor with Stripes. I stopped my credit cards and informed Reception. They were really good. They gave me £50 cash and sent dinner up to my room that night. Even my room keys were in the bag! By this time, Stripes had vanished. I had to continue the search on my own. The stairs to the basement, car park, surrounding area, I looked in the bins ... but to no avail.

In my room I stacked the empty silver platters up against the door. *If anyone uses the keys to break in, they're gonna come crashing down, making the most horrific din!* I was proud of my ingenuity. Little solace though! This was my last night. I tried ringing Stripes to keep him informed, but no answer. I reported my stolen bag to the police and was given a crime reference number.

The next morning, I was determined to catch the same train back on the same seat I'd already booked. I went straight to the customer service desk at the station and explained my situation. Having a crime reference number, I thought they'd be accommodating. But oh no! No way!

Standing at the desk in the densely populated main ticket office, I explained my predicament to the big burly customer serviceman. It was like talking to a brick wall! I was promptly told, in no uncertain terms.

"There's nothing I can do. You'll just have to buy another ticket."

"But my bag was stolen," I replied calmly. "It has all my money, my phone and my train ticket in it." I was sure this was a simple misunderstanding. "I have no money to buy a new ticket."

"Well, you'll just have to get someone else to buy a ticket for you."

"But my mobile has been stolen! I don't know any phone numbers to ring."

"You'll have to get someone to buy you a ticket and then fax a copy to us," was his irritatingly indifferent response. That was it. There was nothing he could do nor was prepared to do and with that, I was dismissed. In retrospect, I think he probably didn't believe a woman would be travelling alone in London and I was putting on some kind of 'ruse'. How rude!

Humiliation, combined with frustration and desperation, flooded over me. It was awful. I almost felt like crying, he was so insensitive! I had a crime reference number for chrissakes! Crazy! I was furious with the man. *What if I'd been a fifteen-year-old kid who'd run away from home, got to the Big City of London, reached Euston Station, had second thoughts, and decided I wanted to go home, then encountered that twat?! They wouldn't have got back home!* I thought incredulously. *This is disgusting!* And with that thought, I decided to write a formal letter of complaint to the railway company.

Fuming with the injustice of it all, I thought, *Hang on a minute. I've already bought a ticket. And I'm certainly not prepared to buy another! I'm gonna get on that train and take my seat anyway!*

Armed with my new resolve, I went to the platform of the train I was hell-bent on getting and asked an official where the train guard was. He pointed to a flag and said, "If you wait over there he'll be there soon."

Grateful for a kind word, I followed the direction he was pointing. Luckily, I found myself at the front of the queue which soon formed behind me. And next in line to me in the queue was a hunky team of rugby players! *Frickin' hell! I'm gonna have to go over all this again in front of all of them!* I thought in dismay.

Fifteen minutes before the train was due, the train guard turned up. I started to explain my situation, but he didn't even let me finish.

"Were you travelling first class or ordinary, Madam?" *Choice words,* I chuckled later.

"Ordinary."

"Go and get yourself a seat in Quiet Coach. I'll see you later."

"Thank you ..." I trailed off. Now I really *did* feel like crying!

He caught up with me near the end of the journey.

"Thank you so much for doing that. Thank you for believing me," I said, reaching for the relevant papers, "Here's my crime number and the list of things that were stolen."

"I see lots of people every day in my job, ma'am, and I can tell the difference between the ones who tell the truth and the ones who are lying," he said good-naturedly, "don't worry about it at all." I felt so relieved ... and to finally get back home! I never got my bag back though.

Later I discovered the hotel had checked their CCTV footage and traced the theft to someone who had come in through the car park, up the basement stairs and had literally crawled around the huge, structured pillar on his belly to sneak round and carefully 'lift' my bag! Preposterous!

We had been sitting in the quietest part of the foyer nearest to the basement stairs. If we hadn't been sitting in that exact spot it would have been impossible for my bag to have been taken. There would have been nothing for him to hide behind. In retrospect, I think I must've been leaning forward pouring a cup of tea or something while it was happening, so hadn't noticed. *How many other times has this happened to some poor unsuspecting person,* I wondered incredulously to myself, *I bet it's been done loads of times before. Far too slick!* "Opportunist thieves!" I muttered under my breath.

I desperately tried to find a replacement for my bag but couldn't. I was gutted. I really loved that bag. I've never been able to replace it; it's irreplaceable.

I couldn't get hold of Justin Stripes the night of the theft. I was very annoyed and disappointed with him! Not only had he not continued searching the basement with me, he'd scooted off real quick when I was reporting my bag stolen at Reception. This is one of the things about leading a secret life; he had to get home in his normal routine. He was committed to his schedule, his habitual routine that covered his tracks.

When he finally answered my calls, we decided we were going to meet up and I was going to *thrash the living daylights out of him!* And it wasn't far short!!!

At that time, fetish accommodation was in very short supply, so that's why we decided to hire the *Purple Palace* in South London. The lady owner lived on the premises and had converted three or four rooms, hiring them out to people in the fetish scene at weekends.

Stripes and I frequented there a few times. I beat the living daylights out of him on a regular basis for as long as my schedule would allow. Justin Stripes isn't his real name, of course. As you know I never divulge real names. No. It's a complete play on words. He always dressed in a striped prison inmate outfit. Every single time he was just in stripes and nothing else. So being 'just in stripes', he became known as 'Justin Stripes'! In all the years I knew him he was never called anything other than Justin or Stripes.

Stripes would always hire *Purple Palace* for the whole day. I would honour my morning appointments, then he would arrive in the afternoon. I thrashed him, then we'd go out for dinner. An interesting experience, watching Stripes squirming on his very sore bottom whilst trying to conduct intelligent conversation. I remember a tricky few moments once when a work colleague came up to talk to him over dinner ... he squirmed even more! Sometimes he'd been thrashed so badly he had to wear adult nappies, to soak up any blood! That was Stripes. Just as he liked it.

Justin Stripes figured a lot in my life after our pivotal, initial meeting. That was just the beginning. I'd often stay overnight at the hotel, and he would sleep on the floor at the bottom of my bed. Very fitting for our dynamic. It suited both of us, especially after a night of the cane. If I woke during the night, I would give him another six of the best!

He'd always come to London whenever he could. We started visiting a new dungeon we'd discovered. Once there I would thrash him, then send him away on a pointless exercise or errand. It allowed him time and space to think about what was going to happen to him on his return! I had him buying Mont Blanc pen refills ... stockings ... nightdresses ... I would make excuses – he hadn't bought the right item, size, colour, being late – then I would thrash him for his incompetence, tardiness ... any excuse on his return! And he loved it!

We had some great times in London and really intellectual conversations over dinner. He's a real gentleman. In fact, years later when I bought the Swingers Club up north, he invested in it. A small loan. I paid him back of course. He even gave his professional advice whenever needed. He was very high up in consultancy and with substantial wealth. A really, really clever man. He was a gem, a real treasure.

The longer we spent time together, the closer and closer we bonded. More and more he opened up to me. Candidly, he explained the reason why he wanted to be thrashed.

"It's my atonement for a past action I'd taken," he'd claimed. As a gentleman he'd taken responsibility for his actions, and taken it to real extremes with the punishments he vehemently requested and willingly received.

This is serious stuff! This is one of many reasons people get into this kind of punishment, this lifestyle, though this is only one such example. I suspect there's many more people around like him.

I only found out because we had formed a relationship and I took the time to listen. I find out about people because I'm interested in people, and I am non-judgemental. Ordinarily, a D/S relationship wouldn't confide in this way; it's not usually that personal, that intimate ... But for me, I'm interested in what makes people tick, and I listen.

Wherever I went, he went. We attended various exciting and thrilling capers of fun, court events ... all variety of caning events. We had a brilliant time over the years. Justin Stripes was going to accompany me to the DomCon meet I attended in LA. However, it wasn't meant to be. It was a shame. The US would have loved him and his capability of taking the cane. After attending one of the many fetish events I held at my dungeon premises up north and meeting other kinksters, he had hooked up and run off with another Mistress! Right under my nose and right on my doorstep!

He wasn't my sub. He was a free agent. But we had spent a lot of time together over the years, purely in a caning capacity of course. We were equals apart from that. There was never any romantic involvement in any way. When he ran off with another Mistress though, I was gutted!

And when they both had the *audacity* to call me asking for my blessing ... *Blessing! What!* We fell out! There'd never been any commitment given by either of us, but I felt so betrayed that he had never even mentioned this burgeoning relationship. He had visited her (a few miles from me), driving all the way from London, many times and never said a word. I had no formal link or expectation of him and from him, but the way he did it ... I was angry and then very sad about the whole debacle. For a long time, he had been a wonderful friend and muse. A lesson there for sure: it's not what you do, it's how you do it.

Later, he bought three Tawses from me, ironic in the fact he'd bought them for me in the first place! He used to buy me loads of equipment. He was very generous like that.

Through a weak, romantic notion, we both lost a good friend in each other, because we both knew we could never go back.

Chapter Four

London; Exploring and Doing More

In the previous chapter, I explained how I had started going to London and stayed over for three or four nights. Well, for one reason or another, the submissive I saw couldn't visit me very often, perhaps only for an hour one afternoon and a couple of hours another afternoon, leaving me with far too much time on my hands. Not wanting to waste valuable time, I thought, *Hey, I can make use of this!* My mind went into overdrive. *What a fantastic opportunity to deepen and develop my BDSM experience!* Under the radar of course!

So, I began contacting suitable, potential submissives I'd short-listed from my previous advertisement I'd prepared for whenever I went to London, then started interviewing them. The eight or nine I interviewed were a mix of experience and inexperience.

One such submissive was a masseur who wanted to have kinky sex. He gave me a massage once; though it was very nice, there was no chemistry there for me. Another was good at building websites, which I thought would come in useful and suit my plans; best thing was, we got on really well. It was fun to have such a diversity of useful, talented, and professional individuals at my disposal.

One guy used to take me to see little-known sites in London, then take me to lunch among the locals, away from the backstreets. This, to me, was the proper London. He showed me the pedestrian tunnel under the Thames that surfaced at Greenwich; showed me the Greenwich Mean Time spot; and took me to see the Cutty Sark. I didn't even realise you could walk under the Thames! That was quite fun.

There was a lovely little café I discovered in Central London in the Theatre District area, I think; it was called *'Coffee, Kink & Cake'*. The ground floor was a fairly ordinary coffee shop with a few tables and chairs and items of 'slight' kinkiness for sale, tucked away in the corner. But if you carried on through to the back of the café and down the spiral staircase, it led to a glorious area where you'd find kinksters hanging out, sitting drinking coffee and eating cake! I absolutely loved that place!

Gradually I built up my knowledge of London and the BDSM scene. Now I had my stable of submissives, my next job was to find a suitable dungeon to use. Eventually I found *Purple Palace* in South London.

It was a detached house that had been converted into part-living accommodation for the house owner and part-BDSM dungeon. It comprised of three or four different rooms, as well as bedrooms for people to sleep over whenever they wanted. I liked the fact it was readily available.

It was a very nice set-up actually. It was on the main London rail network, within walking distance of the station, and came in very useful for several double-domme sessions as well as quite a few single sessions whenever I could slot them in; mainly with Justin Stripes. Stripes worked in the area, so we had much fun fantasising that I would order him to visit me during his lunch hour, he would bring me lunch, then I would give him a good thrashing before he would trot off back to work! And he did!

I also had a good mixture of amateur and professional sessions. The amateur sessions were for me. They were entirely and unashamedly for my satisfaction and enjoyment.

The professional sessions, however, were purely for money. That arrangement was specifically for people that couldn't devote the time they wanted to the lifestyle, who most certainly didn't want the commitment, but were prepared to pay. It was a good and fair exchange.

Whenever I went to London, I always made money. I covered all my costs, and then some! Being self-employed, I was meticulous with keeping receipts and accounts. I didn't want the HMRC having any excuse to dip into my self-employed earnings! Luckily, one of my clients was an accountant who always took care of preparing my accounts for me. Come to think of it, I'm sure I owe him a few canings!

The Purple Palace had been a great starting point for my fledgling career as a dominatrix in London – it was perfect for that – but it was a bit of a trek from Kensington. It was also a trek for my submissives, so I really needed to find somewhere in Central London that could cater for my needs with easier accessibility for all concerned. It made sense.

Eventually, by word of mouth, I found a lovely dungeon just off Tottenham Court Road, a perfect location near the Imperial College Hospital. Situated in a basement, it boasted two rooms and a bathroom. I was lucky enough to make an agreement with the dungeon Mistress, Madam A, who was a Pro-Domme herself. She used to hold her own sessions there, but also used to hire the dungeon out.

I managed to hire the whole dungeon for £150 for a full day in London. The going rate at that time was £50 per hour. A fantastic deal! I really landed on my feet with that one!

I'd also spotted another dungeon near Baker Street which I thought could be suitable. It was quite nice and not far from Baker Street tube station. The owner who rented it out was lovely; a very professional Transvestite (TV). It had a small dungeon room and a school room, but I decided against it in the end. It was more expensive, plus the front door opened straight onto the street and was right next door to a pub! It was way too public for my liking. It was okay in some ways, but didn't have the flexibility I was looking for. It didn't suit me anywhere near as much as the one in Central London.

To find something just off Tottenham Court Road was quite a bizarre find. I delighted in the thrill of thinking people were going about their business, doing their general shopping, while

I was there just below them, administering punishment, in the dungeon, in the basement right under their noses! It was a really nice dungeon in a beautiful old building with lovely big rooms. I liked it very much. *Madam A* used to live in the flat directly above it.

It was so central I could even walk there from Euston if I was feeling fit and the weather was good. If I got a taxi, the taxi cost around £6 which tells you how far it was from the station. It was fantastic! Perfect for me. A lot of people think that London is a huge place, but most places in Central London are quite walkable if you know where you're going. I got to see a lot more of the sights that way.

Once or twice I stayed in the hotel at Euston, just across the road from Euston railway station. It was a beautiful old building. Just beautiful. It was quite cramped, and quite expensive, but it was very convenient for the dungeon. I sometimes walked through the *Fitzrovia* Quarter of London on my way to the 'office'. *Fitzrovia* is one of my favourite parts of London. Close to Central London, packed with lots of old and interesting buildings, yet within close enough proximity to walk over to the train station for me to catch the train home.

Compared to Kensington where I had to take a £20 taxi ride to get to the dungeon, or a transfer on the tube, to be within walking distance was an absolute joy! So quick! Minimal fuss! Easy to get there! Bliss! That's what I liked most when I finished my long days and went to catch the train in the evening. The trains back were usually pretty regular between six and eight o'clock.

I used to enjoy my walks around London. Especially from the dungeon if I'd been whipping Stripes arse, which I tried to do whenever I went! We used to walk back to the station with him carrying my bags and my canes, stop off in a restaurant, usually a nice Italian Restaurant halfway and have a nice meal. Then I would relax on the train journey home. A very pleasant ending to another exciting journey. Sometimes I'd be so excited mulling over the events of my stay, but if I'd had a particularly busy schedule on my trip, the motion of the train would just lull me into such a state, I would doze off until I reached my stop, which thankfully, I never missed once.

I travelled First Class whenever possible. I always used to book my tickets well in advance so I could travel First Class. I discovered if you booked three months in advance, you could travel to London at a very reasonable price. That suited me just fine thank you very much.

Some months when I went to London I would stay over, and some months I just took a long day-trip. But once my client base had built-up to a substantial level, I started going down every month.

It did mean however, that I had to be meticulous in my planning so I knew when I was coming down to London. Funnily enough, that ended up being a bonus for my submissives, and my clients too! Peoples time was valuable. And when I was doing Pro-Domme work, the type of guys I used to see always had their diaries booked up well in advance so they were able to make commitments well in advance. ; that suited them down to the ground. It was perfect all round, win-win.

So, what else did I do in London?

I did used to see quite a few people in my hotel room. Submissives that wanted to come for a spanking session or a light caning session didn't always want the severity of the dungeon and the austere surroundings; some wanted to be in a more domestic environment.

Generally I booked either a large room at Kensington, or was usually upgraded to a Suite, sometimes with separate bedrooms, ideal for my plans. It made inviting clients up to my room so much easier. Initially, for a first meet, I would always meet them in Reception before allowing them into my 'quarters'. Those I knew, I would just give them my room number and they'd come up ... flying under the radar again!

It was customary in those days for submissives to bring their Mistress a gift. I managed to collect an array of very good BDSM toys – whips, floggers, paddles, canes and the like; shoes; perfume ... gallons of it! In fact, eight years later, I've only just finished using the last of it!

The good thing about the hotel at Kensington was it was so huge! People were coming and going all the time. There was nobody with an inquisitive eye wondering what was going on or what I was doing.

It was ideal because my *'Modus Operandi'* was always to keep a low profile in this sort of business. There's all sorts of stories of escorts identifying footballers, musicians, celebrities etc., and the 'kiss and tell' – stories that appear in the Sunday newspaper. One thing I valued and respected about being a Dominatrix was all of this was underground. *Under the radar.*

You just didn't tell people's secrets not and identify them! It simply was not done; these were their secret lives. You heard about situations and events that happened, but you would rarely be able to identify people. Newspapers, the News of the World especially, had a thing about 'outing' people in public. I think everybody can remember Frank Bough being 'outed' for his sexy BDSM-type parties. I think it ruined his television career, actually, which is really sad.

Strangely enough, one of the subs I met and got to know very well in America was one of his friends at that party. People's secrets are people's secrets, and they stay there. That to me is very important.

I remember another big News of the World reveal; an undercover sting of Max Mosley. He used to visit a Dominatrix and she sold her story for £20,000. She did it to pay for her wedding. In the end she never received the whole £20,000, just the first payment of £10,000.

Although I'm writing this book, I have to say, you won't be able to identify any of my clients; unless it's you of course! No, that stays in my head. And that's the only place its staying! Names have been changed or alter ego names used throughout, to protect identities. When alter ego names have been used this has been approved by the owners of their alternative identities.

My word is one of my values. If I say I'm going to do something I try my utmost to do it. I wouldn't divulge any personal information that would identify somebody, but she did it. The dominatrix sold her soul for £10,000.

I felt for Max Mosley. The newspapers blew the whole event out of all proportion. Of course they did! That's what they always did back then. It was outrageous! However, his 'outing' did more for the freedom of being able to have a private life than anybody had ever done: it ultimately saw the News of the World's demise. I think a lot of people can breathe more easily as a result of it, and so they should! It's disgusting what they used to do just to get a story.

People ought to be allowed to have private lives. We all like different things. We all do different things. It's socially acceptable to smoke 'til you get cancer; it's acceptable and even encouraged to drink, to risk becoming addicted and get cirrhosis of the liver; but it's not considered to be acceptable to be caned, which releases endorphins that give you a high. It's so judgemental.

As long as you're not harming anybody else and everyone involved are consensual adults, I really believe society should be less judgemental about things. As a Dominatrix, we always are. Of course, there's the misconception that BDSM is all to do with sex, and sex is a taboo subject in the UK. That's the same pretty much all around the world. Sex *is* a taboo subject. But – sex sells!

Selling sex is one of the oldest professions, and along with being in the Army, sex is one of the oldest professions in the world, yet everybody keeps quiet about it. Such a taboo subject. People love when it's disgusting and smutty. It embarrasses people. I don't know why.

BDSM doesn't necessarily have anything to do with sex. It is sexual, but it isn't anything to do with having sex. Not for me, that is. I wouldn't say that this applies to every Mistress, because there are some Mistresses – not many, but there are some – that do have sex with their clients.

But that's not for me. I've never had sex with a client, nor would I. To me it's crossing a boundary; it's crossing over a threshold into different territory. And in my eyes, *'never the twain shall meet'*. They're separate.

Chapter Five

Steve, Patrick, and Terry

Steve was one of my first submissives; we were both making our very tentative steps together. Whilst I had slightly more practical experience, he had a wealth of fantasy experience. It was a great combination. He was a loyal servant of mine for many, many years. We suited each other, we bonded, and our lifestyles fitted perfectly; that is, until he found love ...

Many people feel they are yearning for something in life but don't know what it is, yet on the other hand, many people yearn for something knowing *exactly* what it is they are wanting! It's often about testosterone. It's one of the main reasons guys watch porn. Men are driven by testosterone. Some men have control of it, some don't; some are unfaithful; some even worse!

Steve had been having yearnings towards a submissive lifestyle for many years. He didn't want to just rush off and have sex with anyone, he wanted to do someone's bidding, and his ideal preference was a curvaceous and voluptuous lady.

He'd confided to me that when he had been a teenager, a group of girls had trapped him in a back lane, pushed him to the ground, pulled down his trousers, and forced him to expose himself. They taunted him and laughed as they pointed at his penis. They humiliated him. He was just at that age where he was starting to get erections, and he found this experience strangely exciting. That, he said, was where it all started.

Over the years he had many, many fantasies. He had bought copious amounts of magazines that reflected these fantasies, and used to take them to work in his briefcase with his sandwiches because he knew his wife would never look in there. That worked out great until someone raided his office while he was elsewhere and left them scattered outside work! Then, when he finally *did* pluck up the courage to 'do something about it' and pushed the boat out, all he did was phone a Mistress to enquire about booking an appointment. That was it. His fantasies never got past the starting block and never grew to any more than that. The excitement of that phone call kept him going for many years.

It wasn't until he had separated from his wife that he decided he would follow his fantasy and make it happen. He contacted me, but for me, at that time, he was too inexperienced. I needed a bit more guidance of what his passion was, what he wanted and what his expectations were. I told him to come back when he had experienced more. So he went away and came back some months later.

We met for coffee, which turned into lunch, and that's when we really hit it off. Steve had his own company and I loved to talk about business. I wasted no time in taking him under my wing as part of my stable. He became my submissive, my 'go to' man. We had so much fun! And we explored so much of the lifestyle: attending events together; going out for dinner; travelling away for the weekend to Rome, then Amsterdam. He even accompanied me to New York and Los Angeles!

As my experience grew and I started undertaking professional sessions all around the UK, I started receiving requests from people from my local area. I didn't have access to a dungeon at that point, but that didn't matter, because Steve offered his office for my use. He had a boardroom, offices, archives, and a reception area. So, at night, after the staff had gone home, he transformed his offices into my 'office' space, and I used to hold my role-play sessions there. They were great fun.

I would instruct the client to go to the local pub and wait in the carpark in a particular spot, which Steve used to jokingly call Madam Rattan's parking space, then Steve would pick them up from there. He used to make them lie face down on the back seat, cover them with a blanket so they didn't know where they were going, lead them into the office blindfolded, then sit them in a chair in reception, instructing them to wait until they were called. We wanted to keep the location secret; at that time there were so many horror stories about people being outed that we were cautious, operating 'Under the Radar'.

We had some wonderful sessions there. I held some of my own, some with *Mistress Torment* (who I will explain about in the next chapter), and a couple of times we even invited another Mistress friend along and had a triple-Domme day, passing the clients between us! What an experience! Everyone loved it; we were all on a massive high! We had a spanking room in reception, facilities to string them up under the fire exit stairs, the archives were set up for humiliation play with dog balls and dishes, and the boardroom was used for a general session. Welcome to the House of Fun!

All went really well until one evening, one of Steve's staff came back into the office to pick something up he'd left behind! *Aghhhh!* There was me, dressed in my red leather corset, black leather skirt and black leather boots; and in he strode! He walked straight past me and into the stores! I moved fast, and hid! He never said anything … and he never came back at night again!

We even filmed several caning clips with bbc-boy – oh boy, did we have some fun! Steve remained my faithful and cheerful servant for many years. He really was a good sport. He used to take part in all the events, even serenading us with a song and dance at every *'Mistress Weekend Break'* we had. He made me laugh so much. It never occurred to him to complain or moan; no matter what I asked him to do, he always did it with a smile. He just wanted to make people happy. He was a great asset to me over the years. Sadly for me, but good for him, he found love with another fetish lady and they ran off into the sunset. I wish them the best life they can possibly have.

Whilst my burgeoning dominatrix career blossomed, I was still working full-time as a Civil Servant and used to travel quite a bit. I got a job on an inter-departmental project based in Blackpool, and it was here I met two very important men in my life.

I used to stay three-four nights per week in a lovely hotel on Lytham seafront, complete with swimming pool, huge rooms and lovely breakfasts. All my evenings were free.

As always when I've nothing to do, I found something. I needed to meet people, so just like in London, I started looking for new friends. That's when I met Patrick. We had met online on the old *Alt.com* site and had been communicating for some time. He loved to write erotica, so we decided to have fun with it. We'd send each other the beginning of a story, swap them over, then the other would add more to it before sending it back again. We had such fun. It went backwards and forwards so many times. The stories got deeper, raunchier ... or more and more hilarious. What a laugh!

This guy had endured a very strict upbringing. Everything around him screamed alpha male – an understatement if ever there was one! He was one of the boys; a real roughie-toughie, the sort you would not want to annoy or 'cross swords with' type of machoism. And what an interesting character! He always turned up in his flashy car with the personalised numberplate. He was intosports, and knew his stuff! He worked in security for a number of important people and was well-known and well-respected in his field.

... and he had a secret. He liked to dress up as a female. He would send me pictures of himself dressing. He had the most wonderful legs, as most TV's generally do. He wore very old style, prim and proper, thick American tan-colour stockings, button-up blouses, formal skirts, and low kitten heels. I could never figure out his dress sense; perhaps it was something to do with the women he grew up with. Perhaps a 'Great Aunt' or something.

We would meet up, then he'd take me out to dinner. He'd never spoken to anyone about his secret before, but over dinner, with me, he would open up and release his inner feelings. It was all welled up deep inside. He also told me that he'd once got involved with a local Mistress, who'd take him shopping and spend all his own credit card on him, then used to tie him up to the bed all night.

He strongly suspected she was taking drugs and wasn't prepared to give up all his power to her. He liked the element of danger, but not that much. He thrilled in her spending his credit card though. She would take his card from him, in front of the shop staff, and spend! Humiliation? Power? Control? Out of control with no power, is the way he explained it, and he loved it! I don't know how anyone else could explain that! I could never see it that way myself.

Patrick and I used to meet regularly for dinner in Lytham, and sometimes he even used to come over to the dungeon to help me with filming sessions. He wouldn't dress in front of anyone though, he could only dress when he felt relaxed, usually when everyone else had left. He was still very, very private in that regard.

Yet, despite being very private, he couldn't stop his tendencies to dress. Regardless of how much he felt it was wrong and how guilty he felt as a result, he still needed it and still craved it. A polarity of extremes to say the least! I do believe that wearing a dress helped balance his life and put some softness back into the hard, controlled nature of his day-to-day life.

He was brought up in this macho world where he couldn't admit to any weaknesses, particularly with his strict religious background. He had the most overwhelming urge to dress up, put on soft silky lingerie and be ultra-feminine; the very opposite of his life. This way, his alter-ego provided him a way of expressing his feelings and more tender side.

Through our regular chats over dinner, he often spoke about his work in America with such familiarity that, unbeknownst to me, he'd planted a seed in my head. That seed was to go to America. He kept saying to me, "Mistress, they'd love you in America. An English Rose. They'd love you there. You should go." And, eventually, I did, as I explain later in the book.

I met Terry through the same alternative website as I did Patrick – as I did most of my first stable of subs. Everyone I met on the *Alt.com* website, known for its BDSM Alternative Lifestyle Personals, lasted years and years. Such was the pull of the site and the type of people who frequented it.

It's still active today, though I think I was using it when it was more in its prime. It's the same site where I met my first 'Sugar Daddy', but they were all sugar daddies to begin with. Some, I discovered, had strong similarities, like Terry and Patrick. I find that quite interesting. Very intriguing.

My first face-to-face meet with Terry was in Lytham. He was a charismatic man, a powerful man; good-looking, well dressed, and liked fast cars, as shown whenever he turned up in his sports car or huge Mercedes. Terry was very personable, yet strangely humble. He knew where he came from and had worked very hard to reach the success he'd achieved.

"Nobody tells me what to do except you," he admitted, "I can't be myself with anybody else. I know we'll be together a long, long time," he'd said with distinct certainty that very first time we met. And we were – ten years or so. We got to know each other very well.

He owned a large firm in a large northern city. His normal life consisted of barking orders at everyone, all day, every day. He was under so much pressure, his staff were under so much pressure, to achieve targets and hit deadlines; he had more than thirty professionals under him. It was a massive company. He wanted to try balance things out a little bit ...

Like my sugar daddies in the past, he used to pay my travel, hotel, food and drink, and expenses every time we met in Leeds. The train station was within walking distance to the hotel – of course! I could also take my car, park it in the basement car park, then take the lift straight up to my suite. Suites were almost the norm these days, such was my regularity ... and loyalty.

I always went to Leeds on Friday mornings. It suited both of us. Terry would visit his relative studying at the university but came to see me beforehand. A perfect cover! I had my Dominatrix appointments Friday evenings and Saturday mornings, then went home. He paid and I used my time the same as I did in London. This is how I met my web manager and *Lady A*. I was always building up my stable and contacts; it would have been crazy not to.

Once he phoned me when I was in Plymouth at the Cinema with my mum. It's not often he would call, so I went outside to take the call.

"I can't stop thinking about what you do to me," he blurted over the phone, "I'm with my wife and all I'm thinking about is you!" Wow! It came right out of the blue! I had obviously got into his psyche. He had been drinking and his true feelings all came tumbling out.

After that he stopped drinking to keep a firm grip. His mind was wandering. This was serious shit! Family, children, business. We didn't even have a relationship! I just tortured him. That was all. We could never have had a relationship. What I did to him was his fantasy. A relationship would have taken the fantasy from the 'bubble' that it was, out into the real world. That would never have worked – not with Terry, anyway.

Terry was from an era where he was the provider; he took on that responsibility as that's just how things were then. It's hard to imagine now, but 50 years ago the social conditioning to do certain things was enormous. Don't live together, get married and have a baby – if not, why not? Being gay was not really talked about, sex education at school and often at home didn't happen, women were frequently hit on at work and no-one thought it wrong (except maybe the recipient), men were pretty much always the leaders and bosses ... the list goes on. It was another era, and still is in some places.

Opening up on that kind of level of deep intimacy without being intimate is potent, powerful stuff. It's all about unearthing, discovering, understanding, and knowing their inner core, and gaining their trust. These men could *never* have admitted their innermost secrets to anyone, not even their partners, if they had them. Their partners had expectations of them being the provider, the 'man', the dominant personality. Knowing their alter ego and seeing them like this, well, the chances of partners seeing them in the same light afterwards were very slim. This is one of the reasons why people have a secret life.

I discovered and unravelled a lot of people I met; opening up a part of themselves to me that never got opened up, not even to themselves. There was a tremendous amount of pressure on men to conform, sometimes to hide from their innermost nature and/or, quite often, to hide from their sexual tendencies. It's different now though. There's been a definitive change in the last ten years; people are becoming much more liberal and open-minded, and accepting.

Another one of my other stable subs used to come visit me from his hometown near Hull. A lovely, quiet, shy man who had been repressed by his parents, he felt awful asking for something for himself. We just talked and talked. He bought me the most beautiful pair of soft and very delicate leather gloves that fitted me perfectly. I still have them to this day; a wonderful reminder of him.

He would always bring me a box of deliciously expensive chocolates, and tucked in the side was a pile of carefully folded notes. I didn't see him for the money, I saw him for my pleasure, and he knew that. It was our arrangement. He had the notes hidden so discreetly. As soon as I discovered them, I wanted to give them back, but when I mentioned them he got embarrassed and stopped coming. When he came back, I tactfully avoided mentioning it.

I had long term relationships with the majority of people I met. That's quite unusual in the fetish scene. Others usually see just one person, or different people all the time. It was a dangerous lifestyle. People could end up dead, marked … any number of things can go wrong, dependent upon the preferences they care about enough to indulge in.

The type of person that sees a Dominatrix regularly is usually somebody that has got a lot more than a relationship to lose; often a position in business or a position in society. They need to be assured of their discretion. That is a core part of being a professional Dominatrix.

Escorts often have a kiss and tell, money-orientated mentality, but professional Dominatrix, the best in their profession, are the ones who would may kiss and tell but NEVER identify publically or privately.

The extent that men open themselves up, whether to unburden themselves or as a form of release, is dependent on the difference between their wants and needs. There's lots of people that might want to be flogged, but there's also a lot of people that need to open themselves up to a *'confidante'* who can help balance their lives.

Chapter Six

London; Twisted Sisters:
Ladbroke Grove Episode; Police.

I love staying at a good hotel. And here I am again, on a Thursday afternoon after checking in, now tucked into this little peaceful haven in Kensington; the then seventh floor Executive Lounge, out on the patio that flanks two sides of the entire building, enjoying my complementary drinks, nibbling delicious food on display for my pleasure as I watch the planes arrive and depart on their flight-path to Heathrow. What bliss!

So here I sit, waiting for my friend *Mistress Torment* to arrive, enjoying the afternoon sun on my face, mulling over the plans we are going to lay out for our Double-Domme sessions the next day and looking forward to a peaceful, secluded, leisurely cooked breakfast ... *ah,* life couldn't get much better than this.

We'd had enough bookings to arrange for the both of us to come down to London on this trip. It made it worth our while. We'd called ourselves *Twisted Sisters* and had enjoyed a lot of fun setting it up. We knew we'd have to think up the right name to advertise as a Double-Domme service. We did have other names we'd mulled over, but for me, the name is the most important part of it; so *Twisted Sisters* was born.

In our Double-Domme persona as *Twisted Sisters, a* key line we wrote in our advertisement or on social media was:

"Welcome to the world of Pain and Pleasure. You receive the pain, we receive the pleasure! Featuring Mistress Torment and Mistress Torture."

The bookings came.

Well, I've come a long way since my first tentative trip to London, I mused as I relaxed more comfortably in the chair. *And all because of an opportune comment to the Hotel Manager.*

I had mentioned there'd been a problem with the bathroom in my room when checking out of the hotel on my first visit. The hotel manager thanked me profusely, probably because I didn't make a scene.

"Email me next time you book," he'd said, slipping his business card into my hand, "I'll see what I can do for you in return." I'd thought nothing of it until my next visit. *Okay,* I thought, picking up his business card, *let's try this.* Lo and behold, he remembered me and the incident! True to his word, he did do something for me: he upgraded me ... and it's been that way ever since. Having an upgrade automatically gave me unrestricted access to the executive lounge. What luck!

I love being upgraded to the Executive Suite floor. They always supply complementary food and drink when available, and a constant supply of tea and coffee. Perfect. As a frequent traveller I soon became a Platinum Card Member and was upgraded whenever I went to a hotel in that chain. I usually was lucky enough to be allocated rooms with free access to the Executive Floor Lounge, thrilled at not having to pay full Premium Rate for the privilege. At London prices this was a significant bonus.

Although spacious and airy in the lounge and patio area, the bedrooms were quite small in comparison. Tonight, my friend and I were sharing a twin-bedded room. We decided on an early night after planning our sessions for the next day.

As soon as our heads hit the pillow, we heard a commotion from the room next door. Someone was using some sort of CB radio. As we listened to more and more dialogue, we figured there were definitely more than two people in the room, and we could hear what they were discussing! It was the police doing some sort of undercover operation in Ladbroke Grove! They had people under surveillance – definitely more than one!

They continued on throughout the night. We thought it really funny at first, very amusing as we both held a glass to the wall to hear more clearly. In reality though, it was all highly confidential. We heard a male and female voice. They were the police! A couple more of the surveillance team turned up later. Wow! This must be a seriously big operation!

As the night progressed, we started to get worried. We were infinitely more than a little concerned! We had a six am humiliation and caning appointment and certainly didn't want the police to hear us. If we could hear them, they could surely hear us!

I tossed and turned through the night worrying. I couldn't sleep. I decided I would ask for another room ... Before I knew it, I woke with a start. We'd slept in!

Too late to change rooms now. We just have to go ahead with it, I thought, though I had my reservations. I wasn't sure if it was possible.

I didn't have a chance to shower in the morning; so, as part of his humiliation session, our client had to lick my dirty, smelly feet, clean ... and between my toes ... the most definitive of power exchange!

If the police could hear us, they're bound to realise we could hear them, I reasoned, so we came to the conclusion they wouldn't say anything. It was in effect, a double-bluff! We heard nothing from the police about our activities. Phew! Later, we thought they must've returned to the police station, or whatever, though we hadn't realised at the time. It wasn't until we walked back to our room later that afternoon that we discovered that the room had been vacated. The door was wide open, and the cleaners were hard at it, what a relief! The law had gone.

The morning humiliation and caning session lasted ninety minutes as arranged, and went without a hitch. It was booked for that time before our client went to court ... he was the ... well, I shall leave it to the imagination what part he played; all I'm saying is, he wasn't the defendant!

We showered, freshened up and discussed the incredible events that had happened during the night over breakfast on the patio. We had heard muffled snippets of conversation about an undercover operation. We just couldn't believe what we'd heard, it was too 'unreal' to be true ... but it was! Refreshed and invigorated, we were in plenty of time for our next session at nine am.

Our usual routine in Central London included having sessions in the London Dungeon just off Tottenham Court Road. I interspersed my solo sessions and continued gathering my 'stable' between our two or three Double-Domme sessions. During that time, I managed to do quite a substantial amount of networking.

I was on the lookout for submissives for my 'stable' in London. I would interview each one in the foyer of the hotel over tea, openly discussing their submissive tendencies and what they would offer in their allegiance to their potential Mistress. The fact other people may be listening in was of no concern of mine. The humiliation was entirely theirs! These people didn't want a relationship; what they wanted was the adrenaline rush, and they would pay.

There are two types of submissive. Those that pay, and those that don't *expect* to pay. But there are many different types of people interested in the lifestyle, or thrill, of being a submissive.

Those that pay cover a wide variety of genres and lifestyles.

Firstly, there's the 'Married Man'. A hectic schedule with very little quality time for themselves. These people have an aching void inside them that their vanilla life just can't fill. These are the people who don't want a relationship, so they pay for a session. It has a beginning and an end. No ties and *no* sex! Some married men believe it's okay to go visit a Dominatrix because there's no sex involved, feelings of guilt are somewhat diminished. They don't feel they're cheating on their wives in this way. And there are many married men whose wife (or partner) does know they visit, how much they need to visit, and as long as they don't know too many details, they accept this hidden part of their partners. Often, they will indulge their partners and try to act out the fantasy for them, but it rarely works as the dynamic has been set already, plus their partners know they are acting, and they often need more. Sometimes it's best to be with an anonymous person who isn't judging you.

Then there's the 'Powerful Man'. This type may own their own business, or perhaps be in charge of a corporate or multifaceted company with a huge number of employees or subordinates below them; spending their whole day telling other people what to do or making key executive decisions. For them, this is their form of escapism, their release valve. Putting themselves into somebody else's hands where they don't have to make a decision whilst being told what to do really helps their life to become more balanced. This is known as 'Power Exchange' (PE). It helps balance their lives and maintain their equilibrium.

Next is the 'Public School' type. They often crave feelings they've experienced from childhood, stemming from public school where they've been disciplined or caned, or they were brought up by a nanny, house mistress or matron. This type often associate feelings of love with corporal punishment, dependent upon their preferred form of punishment. In particular, it was boarding school where these people felt secure, consolidating the primary reason they re-visit caning. It takes them back to that time and space of attention and love.

Another genre of clients are those that can no longer get their adrenaline fix from doing what they used to do as fit, athletic young men; like sportsmen for example …

This does not cover all the reasons why people do it. Some people just want the high they get from the release of endorphins after being caned.

Clients who arrange sessions for an hour or so will pay money. That money gives them the benefit and intensity of a session that provides exactly what they want. This type of session has parameters dictated by them because these people are generally highly intelligent. They can verbally articulate what it is they need or want to try.

Sessions are very expensive for this type of person. A lot of planning is involved to incorporate what they want and satisfy their needs. Bespoke planning of each session to a lesser or greater degree needs to be articulated to the minute detail, and they don't want beginners! They want a highly professional, organised and fine-tuned Dominatrix, exacting to their requirements of how they wish to beg for forgiveness.

I used to receive umpteen enquiries from many people whose eyes were bigger than their bellies. The number of guys who wanted a judicial caning using no safe word, my God! I rolled my eyes every single time I received this request! Many times over! The number was high. I would slowly and carefully explain to them.

"No! I will not give you a caning! I do not know you and I'm not prepared to cane anyone I do not know. I have no way of knowing whether you're capable of taking it or not and I'm not prepared to take that chance!" I wouldn't give a caning without a safe word either! Not unless I knew them *very* well and they had visited me regularly.

Once I had one guy come to me who insisted he would be able to take a full judicial caning, no problem. He was very persistent. Eventually I managed to get him to agree to a thirty-minute quick session in London. He was adamant he would not use a safe word, but I insisted when discussing my terms that I would stop immediately if he said my safe word – which is *"Mercy."*

So, he turned up, bent over the chair; he was very jumpy; and after three light taps with a Junior Rattan Cane, he jumped up and said he had to go! So much for a 'no holds barred' judicial punishment! He actually called me about twenty minutes later and said, "I could have taken more you know." *Hmmm.* My reservations had proven right. He couldn't take it. For him, it was the fantasy he should have stuck to. The reality was simply too much. Admitting it was too much was something he couldn't do either!

If you are to embark in this lifestyle, you *must* be honest with yourself, or you could get yourself into deep water!

I've had many caning sessions and talked with many caning enthusiasts. There was a common thread among quite a few of the men; the fact that they'd been put off from their fantasy by seeing a Mistress who caned them far too hard, without any regard for 'safe words' or limits.

One even made her client lean out of a second-floor sash window and pulled the window down so far that she couldn't hear his pleadings to stop! That put him off for about ten years. This *does* concern me. I always, always left my clients and submissives wanting more; not praying for less! My clients and submissives were 95% men, the remaining 5% women. This balance has changed now.

Some people have a notion that they don't have to pay, at all! But this is impossible. Because everybody pays ... in different ways. There are people who fail to understand this due to their mindset, perspective and/or romantic take on things. These people like to incorporate BDSM into a relationship they are hoping may be more than just BDSM. They genuinely – mistakenly – think they are going to meet the Mistress of their dreams, fall in love and live happily ever after. I'm not saying that never happens ... because it does, occasionally.

I would go to London for three nights wanting to explore the city, but also to incorporate the Domme/submissive (D/s) aspect as well. I had clients that would pay, as well as submissives I was looking out for to expand my 'stable'. I met a few regular people on the scene that I became friendly with. Each of them had their advantages. These were the type that paid in different ways. Win-win remember!

I was happy to have a massage; I needed somebody with a car to pick me up from the station to the hotel and ferry me backwards and forwards to the dungeon after a hard day's caning; I wanted a sub that would take me out for dinner when I was relaxing; I wanted someone to show me the sights of London; I was also on the lookout for someone who created websites ... These people paid by giving up their time, offering their expertise and/or company in all manner of ways that suited me.

I believe the majority of people that need BDSM in their lives are highly intelligent people. It takes a special kind of intelligence to know themselves well enough to understand the need to have their balls tied up so tightly that they hurt; be caned until their bottom bleeds; be gagged, blindfolded, *and* have their nipples tortured! There's no way that an ordinary person would know that kind of subjugation is exactly what they need.

These highly intelligent people balance their lives by doing something so degrading such as licking someone's feet ... mine, for example. How would they know that unless they were super-intelligent? It's often about their fantasy world and living on the edge!

They bark out orders and instructions to people who jump to their tune, then they enter a dungeon ... The Mistress concerned doesn't have to be a svelte, beautiful woman, though she can be. It's all about someone who understands their core, their essence, their mindset. They want a role reversal, to be barked at, to be treated like dirt, to be whipped 'til they cry.

There are some individuals who want to mix all that with sex and there are some Mistresses that will accommodate, though not many. A Mistress of the 'Old School' would be highly unlikely to entertain that.

Chapter Seven

London; sklavos: Slave on Loan

Sklavos was a foreign slave living in London who came to me on loan. I first noticed him advertising for adventure on the *'collarme'* website. He had a long-term Mistress, *Lady Eliza,* who had relocated to Scotland from London, and as a result they rarely got to see each other.

Missing the interaction between them, sklavos was given a task to set about finding himself a Mistress that he could serve, who was in London. That's when I first met him, and took to him straight away.

I liked him a lot. He had very strong ideals about being a slave. He also had a very, very, important job working for a very large institution. His job involved him travelling a lot; to places as far-flung as the Far East and the USA. He was very clever – too clever, one might say. He needed a release. He needed to be treated with disdain and contempt and to be treated like a slave; to do whatever his Mistress decided, however degrading or humiliating that may be.

We used to meet every time I came down to London, which was usually about once a month. He would pick me up from the station, a godsend! It was great! It saved me getting a taxi and hanging around. He used to be waiting for me on the platform by my carriage, ready to trot along behind me carrying all my suitcases, canes, everything – fantastic!

He would take me to the hotel in his lovely 'to-die-for' expensive, sleek, fast black car, then he'd carry my bags upstairs to my room after checking-in. Once he'd unpacked my bags, he would then set to work rubbing my feet ... he enjoyed foot worship. It was most relaxing. He would also massage me. He'd do anything I told him to, really. If I told him to lie down in the reception area of the hotel and roll on his back like a dog, he would do it.

I remember one London visit with *Mistress Torment*. She had gone out for the evening to the theatre, and I had instructed sklavos to worship and rub my tired and aching feet. He was laid out on his front attending to my feet (licking, kissing, and rubbing) and *Mistress Torment* came back in. She had forgotten something. She opened the hotel door and without a word, went to her bedside table, stepped over him to retrieve her phone, then promptly strode back out! He just carried on without a pause; and she had totally ignored the fact he was grovelling at my feet, like it was the most normal thing in the world ...

I had lots of fun adventures with sklavos. Anything I wanted to do, he would do with complete deference. He used to call me *Ma'am* and take me out to dinner in very posh restaurants. He'd even take me to the places he frequented in his 'normal life'. He was good company and a very intelligent man. Yet, at these restaurants, for a bit of subtle humiliation, degradation and letting him know where he was in my food chain, I would order his dinner; he could not start till I allowed him to; I would drink wine, he was allowed water; I would season his food and he would eat appreciatively, including the dessert.

He also used to take me to his office in the evening and beg me to sit at his desk, then he would crawl underneath it and worship my feet. The security guards doing their checks must have thought we were having an affair! How wrong they were!

We'd drive around London and go to see different things. sklavos had a super-fast car and, interestingly, he often used to get stopped by police in those days. He wasn't black but wasn't white either. It was the time when police had a predisposition to stop foreign drivers. He used to love to drive fast. Difficult in London at any time, day or night, but he did love to put his foot down hard for about 200 metres and then slow right down to avoid the speed traps ...

At one point I'd been looking to buy a hotel on the other side of Bristol. I flew to Bristol, and he drove up the M4, picked me up from Bristol Airport, then drove me all over Somerset.

He accompanied me to look at the hotel and was really good in giving me an unbiased opinion. Interestingly enough, I remember the lady in charge of showing us around mainly talking to him throughout the viewing. He would just say, "Sure, sure, sure, sure, sure, sure, sure ..." He paid for that afterwards. The constant repetition of *'sure'* – it drove me nuts! The grovelling he had to do to make it up for it; the dinners, the flowers, the jewellery ... plus I whipped his hide until he whimpered!

We drove all over Somerset; Cheddar Gorge, and some wonderful local places of interest, while we were checking out the area. It was a lovely day, we were having a great time and in sklavos' car it didn't take long to get anywhere. I wasn't driving and I didn't care. I could sleep if I wanted. I could literally do anything!

We decided to stay overnight somewhere, then continued our trip along the north coast down to the south coast of Devon to see my friend, *Mistress Eve of Devon,* while we were out and about. She really lived the lifestyle; a friend from *FetLife* who also had a residence near Bristol to escape to, purpose-built for fetish fun. It was lovely seeing her again. She is such a delightful Lady, always a pleasure to be with.

I had a lover back in London whom I introduced to sklavos. I would have sklavos be the 'fluffer', then when he'd done my bidding, I would send him to kneel in the corner of the room, facing the wall, hearing our very loud, very vocal sexual noises, and not being allowed to look. All he could do was listen. Sometimes, though, if I wanted him to, I would allow him to take a video of our wild and passionate lovemaking. And it *was* wild!

sklavos came to *Night of the Cane* with me once, as well as to other events, including the *'FemDom Break'* held on a farm in Somerset, one year, and it was just before Christmas. That's when I had sub steve as well as sklavos; it was also the same time that I met *Mistress Sapphire,* an incredible woman whom I will *never* forget!

I kept my distance at first. Being new on the scene and new at the Fem Dom Society (an exclusive & very private group of Dominant lifestyle ladies and their subs/partners), I hadn't known what to expect and this wonderful lady, with her standoffish and gruff persona, well, in my eyes she deserves the best that life can offer. It wasn't until two days into the event that we got the opportunity to become better acquainted, sitting over dinner at the huge dining table. She had mentioned she liked horses – well, that was it! Something we had in common. We started chatting and never looked back.

This lady always helped me whenever I wanted advice. She always knew the right way to do things, how to treat people, and what a woman! Beneath that stern demeanour lay an absolute heart of gold, 24 carat! The work she does for charity you would not believe! Many people had an influence on me, many people helped me along the way, and there were many that had a very big impact on me, but *Mistress Sapphire* is very special to me.

The *FemDom Break* was great! All the Mistresses would meet dressed in all their finery; corsets, boots, leathers and whips. Dinner was always prepared and served by the slaves. It was the stuff fantasies are made of. There were usually around six Mistresses from all over the UK, who all had different vested interests, so the mix was wonderful, and the chat was amazing.

There would always be fun and games in the evening. Games such as clingfilming slaves, who then crawled all over the floor like maggots ... a little race ... as well as all sorts of other party games. We had a caning competition, whipping competition, fancy dress competition ... Ahh, those were the days. Happy days, happy days indeed. A lovely weekend break for everyone. sklavos and steve really enjoyed it as well and became firm friends. They had a great time. I had lots of lovely photos taken of them.

I wanted to own sklavos. I wanted him to be a bit more than on loan. I liked him and I could see him fitting into my life very nicely. He was so, so accommodating and he did it all with such deference. But more than that, he had a brain and one that worked overtime. He opened my mind to a world of different things I didn't understand; climate change, foreign culture, medical research, the USA ... But his Mistress wouldn't give up the rights for me to own him.

Once, I remember, he told me he wanted me to kidnap him. He wanted me to keep him locked up for a couple of months; make him my slave, but it's another thing him disappearing off the face of the earth!

He appeared to be deadly serious about the whole thing! I told him I couldn't do it. I could not take him away from his job. A very important job. Very important. I couldn't take him away from his family either!

I often wondered whether the reason behind the *'kidnapping'* idea was sklavos merely being so super-intelligent and having such complex issues to deal with, and the simplicity of being a slave was the only way that he could balance his life. Because ... yes, I know people go missing ... but you can't just kidnap somebody! It's crazy! To keep them locked away?! What?! It would have made a monster of me. The implications were just mind-blowing! It didn't bear thinking about!

My win-win motto definitely applied here because I knew it was just never going to happen. Playing the Mistress game is great, living the Mistress life is fantastic, but this was going a few more steps down the road. Way, way too far for my liking. Far too dangerous! However, talking about it kept him happy. It was his fantasy, a form of daydreaming, I suppose, his way of daydreaming. What a strange life we live.

Chapter Eight

Cheshire; Mistress Chastity; Rich Client

In the first year or two of embarking on my career as a Pro-Domme, it was clear that a lot of people were desperate for some sort of domination but were unable to meet in person for whatever reason.

They tended to either live a long way away; were married; had a busy work schedule and couldn't take time out to visit; were in denial; or not brave enough to take the plunge. A myriad of personal reasons.

But once the need is there, it's always going to be there. There is only regret for the things you wished you had done.

A large proportion of people just couldn't take that step; to take the plunge and embrace domination into their reality for whatever reason; but they still had that craving, that fantasy. That's when they often turned to being dominated online.

A trend that is very popular, very popular indeed, is orgasm denial. Control and domination could be achieved by denying the recipient/submissive an orgasm. It was a combination of all these reasons why I created *Mistress Chastity*.

I had quite a lot of fun being *Mistress Chastity*, one way or another. I used to do online domination for people and never once showed my face as I never had a webcam and frankly, I had no idea how to get one to work, this was eons ago in the IT world where things move so quickly, nowadays they are built into your lap top! Then the camera was sat on top of it! Although I often had them performing on webcam for me, they didn't even know who I was. Maybe that increased the excitement. I could have been anybody!

I arranged 'monthly packages', and people used to pay around about £100–£150 per month for my online package deal. I would give them instructions, then we'd have some fun. People enjoyed that.

One of my clients was an airline pilot who I could only contact when he was 'on leave'. He flew for a very large airline. He really struggled with his feelings. They had been suppressed for so long.

I also had another client contact me saying he wanted to meet me face-to-face but at the moment couldn't, so online domination would do for now. He actually transferred a year's payment of almost £2000 to pay for my online services instead of paying the monthly fee.

I think his main priority was he wanted the attention he wasn't getting from his wife. He definitely craved a bit of tender loving care (TLC) from somebody else. He was in his fifties, and his fantasy was orgasm denial.

We built up a nice rapport over a few months and during that time, he told me things which, quite frankly, I just didn't believe. He said, "Do you know where the Golden Triangle is in Cheshire?"

"No, I've never heard of it."

"It's where the richest people in the UK live. That's where I live."

"Oh, right," I said, then thought to myself, *Okay, here we go!*

Our relationship progressed to the point where he said he wanted to see me face-to-face. "I don't have time to come to see you. Could you come to see me?"

"Well yes, but it'll be expensive because I'm not gonna travel there and back in a day, so I'll have to stay overnight. There'll be accommodation, travel expenses ..."

I thought it through first. With the hotel, travel expenses and a session with him, I worked out I was going to charge him £450 all-in. We're talking about more than ten years ago here.

The arrangement suited me; I love travelling anyway. *I can see others while I'm there,* I decided, *Yes, I can do this.*

"Okay," I said, "£450. You'll need to pay me a deposit of £250 because I have to book the hotel."

"No problem," he'd said. And he paid the deposit. I thought, *Okay, he's paid the deposit so the intention is there,* So I booked into Mottram Hall, a hotel in the golf triangle that features a lot in the *Real Housewives of Cheshire.*

I didn't book a train ticket because I thought I would get one on the day. I'm glad I waited, because the day before the meet, he cancelled.

"I'm sorry I can't see you tomorrow. Something urgent has come up. I've got an urgent appointment with a client."

"Fair enough. Happens all the time." I said understandingly. *Well,* I thought, *he does have to earn money. His pleasure can't come before earning money.* This happened three times altogether. Three times he paid me a deposit, and each time, he cancelled.

I'd been speaking to Reservations at the Hall, explaining the situation; that I was coming for a business appointment, but the client kept cancelling. They were very accommodating about it. So, I actually only had to book the room once and they just kept changing the dates for me. They were really good. However, the arrangement with the Hall wasn't an open-ended thing. Although they were accommodating about making a couple of changes, they weren't prepared to keep changing the dates indefinitely.

So, knowing I'd be attending a '*FemDom Weekend*' in Somerset with my chauffeur and sub, Steve, and realising it would be quite easy for us to detour on the drive back, I booked the hotel on a Saturday night as a stop-over, then contacted my client.

"Look. I'm coming over your way and staying close by. If you can make it for a coffee Saturday night or Sunday morning, that would be great! If not, I'm there anyway."

"Yes! Yes! Yes, I'll make it on Sunday morning," he replied excitedly, "I'll definitely be able to make it then. You'll recognise me easily enough. I'll be in my Rolls Royce. It has personalised number plates." I thought, *Right … okay*. I didn't believe a word of it! Not a word!

Sunday morning came. steve and I had our breakfast before I returned to my room to await my client's arrival. As it happened, my hotel room was right next to the car park, overlooking the road into it. Ten minutes before the allotted meeting time, sitting in the hotel room thinking he's not going to turn up, a Rolls Royce drove past with *that* personalised number plate. I couldn't believe it! I was absolutely gobsmacked.

I walked across to the car park where we'd arranged to meet, and he invited me to sit inside his car. We had a lovely chat for fifteen or twenty minutes, and then he left.

That was so thrilling, because I never believed anything he'd said about living in the *Golden Triangle* and having this posh car with personalised number plates. Yet it all turned out to be completely true! It just goes to show, you never, never can tell. He really did live in the *Golden Triangle* in Cheshire! That was amusing.

After a while, everything went quiet with him. It often does in these kinds of situations. People get strong, absolute urges and needs to be dominated, and then, for whatever reason in their life, the pressure, the urgency subsides then disappears. Such was the case with him.

To be truthful, on this occasion he disappeared because I fell out with him. He had become quite possessive with me, and for whatever reason he decided he wanted to buy me a gold locket to keep a key to his chastity device in, which I would wear around my neck. So I said, "Okay, that's fine, but I don't wear gold anymore. I only wear silver or platinum. I've got no gold jewellery at all. I've changed all my jewellery."

"Right. I'll look for one," and off he went, hunting through all these online auction sites for jewellery and kept coming up with these antiques; beautiful lockets. Sapphire. He wanted sapphire set in gold. He actually bought me one! He spent £1000 on this locket! A thousand pounds! I was amazed. But he couldn't find a platinum or silver equivalent. He kept on and on, wanting me to have this gold locket. I refuse to wear gold jewellery anymore, so I kept saying to him.

"I'm sorry, I don't wear gold jewellery. I can't accept it." In the end, he got in a strop about it and flounced off! That was it. I never heard from him. But I knew he'd be back. Of course he would!

True to my prediction, a couple of years later he came back. He wanted to meet me. It was the same old, same old story, except he didn't live in Cheshire anymore, he lived in Scotland by a loch. Well, that suited me just fine, because I used to visit Glasgow once a month anyway, mostly to administer CP to some very unruly and objectionable recipients! Generally, they were allegedly sent to me by their Aunt, Great Aunt, nanny ... or even their wife, with a – perhaps forged – letter explaining why. It all adds to the fantasy and the build-up, which is oh so important! Sometimes I used to use a cane on them, and often, a Lochgelly Tawse.

There are many types of Tawse around, but the real authentic punishments are undertaken with a genuine Lochgelly Tawse made by JJ Dick; a very valuable item now. I am lucky enough to own two! One, interestingly, has a natural curve in it, with teeth marks on the end! The curve is because it used to be carried around by teachers over their shoulder under their gown, so they could whip it out quickly to reprimand their pupils.

Corporal punishment was prohibited in all state-supported education in 1986. The prohibition was extended to cover private schools in the UK at different times; England and Wales in 1998; Scotland in 2000; and Northern Ireland in 2003. It was outlawed in schools following a 1982 ruling by the European Court of Human Rights that such punishment could not be administered without parental consent.

Anyway, I digressed a little there, started thinking about Scotland and its long history of being hard on its pupils. So, on this particular trip, I'd planned it so I could have my day in Glasgow, catch the train to Edinburgh to meet up with one of my other subs, then catch a train to the nearest station to where he lived, further up the north of Scotland, and he would meet me at the station. He had a beautiful little cottage in a little hamlet on the loch side, a lovely little lochside village.

He took me out to dinner in a restaurant *James Bond* had been to. I was duly impressed, of course; fine dining always impressed me, although in this instance it wasn't fine dining. Not good at all! What didn't impress me was he drank. He drank and then he drove home. I really was not impressed with that! He wasn't roaring drunk, but I do value my life. He drove home. I was aghast!

When we got back, I went straight to bed and refused eye contact with him; got up in the morning, spoke to him only briefly, then promptly asked him to take me back to the station, explaining in no uncertain terms that I valued my life and I wasn't prepared to entertain somebody who was prepared to drink and drive! He was very annoyed, I can tell you!

The submission he wanted to give me was conditional. Of course, when clients are paying, it is nearly always conditional, but this was based on what *he* wanted *me* to give, and I didn't want to risk being in an accident or worse with a drunk driver. Don't get me wrong, he was prepared to pay handsomely for it, no doubt about that. He wanted me to tell him what to do in certain departments, but he certainly didn't like me pointing out to him about his drink driving! It ended our relationship for good. I never heard from him, nor saw him ever again.

Oddly enough, it reinforced a good lesson: the fact that money can't buy you everything. A lesson I'd already learned in my life. I've discovered that people with money – the rich, and the famous too – can be quite arrogant.

Every good Mistress gets her super rich and/or famous client(s). You'd be amazed and gobsmacked who some of them are. And believe me, they come from *all* walks of life! The super clients don't jump into having sessions with the new and beautiful ladies who set themselves up as Mistresses to earn some 'easy' money. No. These super clients watch and research, then watch and wait. They have too much to lose to get caught out like footballers on a boozy night out.

Choosing the right Mistress for them can change their lives and enhance their quality time. Big time! They gain a *confidante*. Someone they can trust. Someone that's often greatly lacking within their circles for sure!

So, that was *Mistress Chastity*. She was quite a popular little Mistress. Quite hard-working; in the background, under the radar. I had quite a lot of fun with her, going online when I wasn't doing other things. For me, however, all this was work. Enjoyable, but work nonetheless.

Chapter Nine

Leeds; Terry; Practice Makes Perfect

There's more to be said about Terry, one of my oldest subs. To be honest, he wasn't a sub; he was a masochist masquerading as a sub. Pure and simple, he was a masochist.

A submissive has a character that gets pleasure from pleasing people; a masochist will often play that game so they can get their pleasure from pain, which in turn releases endorphins. Many masochists don't have the time nor the inclination to pretend to be submissive, and they usually have paid sessions. That makes for a cleaner and more honest transaction. Some masochists do not feel they can ask for exactly what they want, so mask it as if they are submissive; another example of social conditioning and men having such pressure to do things in certain ways.

What is interesting nowadays is that more and more women are coming forward; it's not just men that are admitting their secret yearnings.

I operate under two mantras: SSC, *Safe, Sane, Consensual*; and RACK, *Risk Aware, Consensual Kink*. It can be argued that doing what we do cannot be safe, however, crossing the road is not always safe either. It's safety, but an entirely different level. Is it sane to practise this? Who knows? It's often perceived as very subjective, and dependent on the degree of level of play. That's when RACK kicks in. Everyone involved and participating is well aware of the risk and consents anyway.

Masochists can visit a Pro-Domme for many differing reasons. I know a guy in the US who used to be (in his words) a beach bum and used to get his adrenaline rush from surfing. As he got older and was unable to surf, he turned to BDSM play to fulfil his needs.

Another whom a Mistress friend of mine used to cane regularly had been discharged from the Special Forces on the grounds of ill-health caused whilst in the line of duty and could no longer get his adrenaline fix from Special Operations. The pain from the caning gave him a buzz that released endorphins and helped mask and manage the extreme pain he suffered daily along with coping with the Post-Traumatic Stress Disorder (PTSD) he'd been exposed to.

I even had a client who was eighty-nine years old! A professor who lived in another country. Each time he flew over he 'popped in' for a thrashing. It helped to level his world.

Terry, I got to know right at the very start of my journey of BDSM and Mistress-ing. He was one of the first people I met and stayed in contact throughout my journey in the Pro-Domme world.

He was a lovely man, still is a lovely man, I'm sure. He lived over a hundred miles away and would drive up in his Porsche or Mercedes to see me for sessions in the chambers at the dungeon. Sometimes he even picked me up from my home – bet the neighbours wondered what was going on! I didn't bother about gossip. He was one of the few people I ever trusted to know my address. I trusted him, but anyway, it was a two-way street because I knew where he worked, so it was never a concern for me.

The sessions I had with Terry were definitely that of a masochist nature; I would cane him then torture his nipples. And he would always get an erection (it wasn't automatic that everyone got an erection, but many did, especially when you found out what exactly did turn their pain into total pleasure!).

He loved his nipples being twisted and got his sexual fulfilment even just fantasising about it. He also liked being blindfolded. It heightened his excitement and arousal. He was always keen on being filmed and used to bring his own camcorder and tripod to every session. He would take it home, make a copy for me to keep, then bring it with him on his next visit. Different people just like different things, I guess.

I remember in one session at the dungeon I used to rent on occasion (this was before I bought it) … I used to sneak Terry into the building discreetly, because he didn't want to be seen.

The caretaker/cleaner at the venue had seen his flashy car so often, he was itching to get a look at the guy. One day we were having our session in our normal space, and he opened the door. Luckily Terry had his back to him – well, he was tied to a chair ...

Immediately I bounded over and pushed the cleaner out, shouting, "Bill! We haven't gone yet!" I practically slammed the door right in his face!

"Ooh, sorry," he said, "I was just checking the rooms. I thought I'd forgotten to clean it."

"Well, wait till we're gone please!" I shouted after him.

"Yeah right!" I seethed under my breath, after checking he'd gone and moving away from the door once I knew it was safe.

Terry just said, *Bloody cheek!*" and I carried on whipping him and tweaking his nipples! That was funny, and actually quite exciting, the thought of nearly being caught ...

Every month when we met in Leeds, I would catch the train and stay at a hotel with an underground car park. That way I could jump straight into the lift from the car park to whichever floor I was on, so I didn't have to walk past the Bar and Reception area. That was useful for him too. That way we were both under the radar!

Hotel chain bedrooms are pretty much standard. Most of them seem to have the same sort of chairs, but in this particular hotel, the bedrooms were equipped with a quite low, soft chair. Every time we went to Leeds, I tied Terry to it. Exactly the same way, every time. I practiced making pretty patterns tying up his cock. The stiffer it was, the better it was. Tying his cock and balls ... it always looked pretty, every time. Sometimes I added bows and bells, and I always took a photo so he could see later what he could only feel at the time.

Blindfolded, nipple clamps on, tying his cock and balls and sometimes whipping them with my mini suede floggers; Terry used to enjoy it all. Every month, the same thing. He used to say to me, "Nobody ever tells me what to do at work, nor anywhere else, apart from you." He used to be in charge of a lot of people. Professional people.

And every time, he recorded our sessions. Every time. Without exception. Later he told me why: he said he used to sit in his own office at the top end of the office floor, presiding over everybody, while watching his DVDs of us together. Obviously on silent! His vocal ability was much to be admired! Everybody used to think he was working away. Instead, he'd be enjoying himself, watching us! He used to get up to all sorts … oh dear! That used to tickle me. He was a very powerful man.

Once, Terry came down to London on his birthday to see me. He used to have this little game where he'd say to me, when he was all blindfolded and tied up, "Please, Mistress, can we have your top off?" And he actually meant, *'Would I take my top off?'* Oh dear! Big mistake! Yes, he got severely reprimanded for that, which I think is why he did it. But I think it was his subtlety as well. Very occasionally, I did take my top off and would smother him with my breasts. Not very often though. Only as special treats when I felt he deserved it. Like birthdays!

Was he a masochist? Definitely! Masochist in a different way to Stripes? Definitely! A very private masochist all the same though. Why did he do it? I think that his life was so unbalanced. He was in charge of a lot of people. He had a lot of stresses. He was running a multi-million-pound business; the stresses involved must have been enormous. He had to make decision, after decision, after decision, after decision.

But he was also conflicted. He knew what he so clearly enjoyed and needed, but thought it was wrong. He struggled for balance in his life, going without it for a while. So, when he came to me, I tied him up. I put his blindfold on him. Often, I gagged him as well. And there was nothing he could do about it. He was completely helpless, which was a complete role-reversal for him from his day job.

Trussed up like this he wasn't making any decisions. He wasn't making the decision of what would happen to him. He wasn't making any decisions about how things would move forward, work plans or anything. He just totally relaxed. Chilled. He didn't know what the hell was coming, and I feel that helped him balance his life. That's what I think anyway.

I feel that is something many people under-estimate. The overwhelming urge to remove themselves from the pressures and stresses of day-to-day work can be powerful. The fear of being caught or 'outed' is huge, yet this inner 'pull' can be stronger than the fear itself. And so it is.

It's difficult to explain. We all understand how testosterone can consume people to behave differently. The people themselves may not like this aspect of doing the things they feel they shouldn't be doing, but they do it anyway. And in the cases I've encountered, they do understand it. Some just can't fight it, and some just learn or find a way to cope with it; like getting up to shenanigans with a Mistress. Few people understand the reasons why people do it, but *so* great must be that pull, that desire to find balance, for those that take the plunge, and follow it through.

Terry was very loyal when we were together. He was a very loyal man. He told me in the early days we would be together for a very long time, and he was right. We remained that way for a good few years. When I say together, I mean together in the loosest possible sense, as we weren't in a romantic relationship. It lasted until he had a serious accident which stopped his visits and rendered him unable to communicate easily or privately; it was most distressing. Such a lovely man. Lovely.

Chapter Ten

London; Lady A

Lady A burst onto the scene in a 'blaze of glory'. She had started posting on the *Informed Consent* website. And she posted *a lot!* She had a lot of opinions. She was very intelligent and always formed a good solid case in her arguments about things. She also caused a lot of controversy on the scene through being so outspoken; but I got on okay with her.

I'd actually first met up with her on one of my trips to Leeds, which is where she was based. One of my clients used to visit me at the hotel Friday afternoons until about six o'clock, so normally I'd be twiddling my thumbs on a Friday evening with nothing to do. So, on one such visit, I invited *Lady A* over, just to get to know her really; to put a face to the name in this small, tight knit, secret, and very private community.

She was quite a dynamic lady. She ran *Kinkdom*, a monthly Fet Fayre/Market during the day that transformed into a dungeon party in the evening. *Kinkdom* had begun in Halifax before re-locating to Huddersfield and had run successfully for about nine months or so but, as far as I know, *Lady A*, with *ZakRLee and Eric Stanton* (both legends and extremely experienced scene leaders), only ran it a few times. After that, it closed for one reason or another. Something happened, though I'm not sure what. They probably lost the venue. That was often the case with kink events.

Yorkshire seems to be a hotbed of spanking good fun. There used to be a legendary event called *'Nemesis'* in the Huddersfield area; a very popular, well run, underground event, again, by invite only. I was lucky enough to get an invite, then continued to have an open invite for every single one after that. This event was also run by experienced and skilled fetish enthusiasts, including *Zak*.

The event was held in a small industrial estate that was difficult to find. On leaving the main road, you were quickly waved in by two burly security guards, who advised you to park round the back out of sight, and who then escorted you with torches to the main door and checked you in.

There was a story that during one *Nemesis* event someone was taken ill, so ill that someone had to call 999. While waiting for the ambulance, everyone rushed around covering up the fetish equipment then hurriedly dashed out of the way. Thankfully, the patient was treated in a private room next to Reception, so the paramedics didn't actually go through the venue itself. The 999 responders were completely professional and were only interested in their patient, who fully recovered and returned to tell the tale! It was rumoured that a couple of months later one of the paramedics applied to join!

Lady A purchased an end terraced property with a basement in Yorkshire, near Halifax way. I can't remember exactly where, I just remember it was somewhere off the M62. Anyway, she lived in the house and converted the rest into kink accommodation to let out. It seemed to work quite well, as far as I know.

It was in quite a remote rural hamlet, in a block of about six terraced houses, all with basements, situated on quite a steep hill. She had made an entrance through the basement for their own private use and lived on the ground floor. The upper floors, catering for the kink-friendly weekend accommodation, could be accessed from the front door. It was cosy and well kitted out for a weekend of kinky fetish play.

So, on this particular Friday evening, I met up with her and we became friends. *Lady A* was transgender. Instead of going through the usual route of living for a year or two as a female, she had told me as we were sipping our cocktails, when she was still legally male, and had made the decision to change her sex, she just wanted it done and over with as quickly as possible. She said she had borrowed money from her parents to pay for her private operation and confided that she didn't know anybody in the kink scene at that point.

Apparently, she'd had her operation and basically lived her recovery through social media, where she became friends with a kink guy who took her under his wing.

I got the impression he'd supported her a lot through all the downtimes and helped her get through it all. He did a lot of good for her, because she no longer had to go through it alone. From what I can understand about the journeys of transgender people, one of the problems is that they don't have people to talk to and it's quite a lonely place to be. That's because a lot of people just don't accept them for what they are … not even their families accept them, understand nor even *try* to understand, which is shocking! And sad.

These differences that people have … you know … they love their families unconditionally, and yet some things really just drive a wedge between families. Families and so-called loved ones, well, they just don't understand. They can't get their heads around it; then they don't tolerate it and then they break off relationships, which I think is really sad. We're all entitled to feel what we feel … and if we don't feel we're in the right body, for whatever reason, why the suffering? It shouldn't be happening. Not in this day and age.

The kink and fetish scene are very accepting of most people. They tend not to judge and are mainly a very friendly community where people are generally welcomed with open arms. For people that may have opened up to others and been rejected or marginalised because of their alternative sexuality or kinks, the scene is a warm and welcome place to be, with respect being at the heart of everything. Well, that's my interpretation anyway.

So, *Lady A*!

As I said, there we were, sitting having a few drinks together, chatting away having a wonderful conversation, when she mentioned she had a few people in London she would like to see but couldn't afford to go down there, so I piped in, "Well, come down with me. I go down to London three or four nights at a time. You're very welcome to stay in my room." At that point, when I used to go to London, the hotel usually gave me a suite, so it had two bedrooms anyway. I've generously invited people over for a couple of drinks before, not really expecting anybody to take me up on the offer, but she did!

She came down to London and well, actually, she also gave me one of her clients. Her client was a caning enthusiast who lived outside London in Surrey and held a very prominent legal position in the city. He lived an opulent life for sure, because, when he collected me from the hotel and drove me to the house, we drove past a lake, a tennis court, a lean-to barn complete with boats, a bowling green, croquet lawn, swimming pool, stables and a huge garage with a flat over ... and that was before we reached the beautiful landscaped gardens!

It was hard not to be in awe. Amazing! It was all very mysterious and exciting! He didn't want lots of strokes of the cane; I very quickly learned that he wanted more than mere chastisement. I thoroughly enjoyed it, but he didn't come back to me. He was looking for a Dominatrix that had a different set of skills than mine. Ah well. It was worth the experience anyway.

The day *Lady A* came down to London was the day after I'd arrived, as I remember. I had already left the hotel that morning for my normal 'day at the office'. I had a day lined up at the dungeon and went to my appointments and to mix and mingle with people.

As the dungeon was so central, it was a good place to be. I had a couple of appointments in the morning – I think I was doing judicial caning training, and had a bite to eat with the editor of my website – and appointments in the afternoon, with one of my enthusiasts calling in on his way home from work to receive a darn good 'over the knee' (OTK) spanking before running me back to my hotel. That was the life! Chauffeur driven in Central London made things so much easier!

However, when I got back to the hotel, *Lady A* was in a completely different room! The room I had booked, the suite that I'd had, wasn't acceptable to her. She'd put in a complaint at Reception – she'd actually got the room changed, and my belongings along with hers had been packed up and moved by the hotel staff! I was absolutely mortified!

I'd been coming to London for a couple of years. I'd quietly got on with my business, sometimes seeing my clients in the hotel room, sometimes at the dungeon I hired, and nobody was any the wiser about what I did. Never once did I complain – about anything! I never created any ripples, apart from when my bag got stolen … never. I gratefully accepted all the upgrades that they gave me; expensive rooms on the Executive floor, which ultimately led me to suites, which was wonderful.

Lady A came along and created hell! I mean she … what can I say?! She liked being the centre of attention. If things were going quietly, she obviously liked to make a scene. Anyway, I can tell you, I never invited her to London again … absolutely not! I suppose you would call her a Drama Queen! To be fair, lots of Dominatrix are! I am not; I quietly go about my business and then leave, no fuss, no noise, no problems, Under the Radar!

My '*Modus Operandi*' is, and always has been, to "*fly under the radar and not create ripples.*" She'd created a tsunami, in my opinion!

Anyway, last time I heard, she'd moved to Europe and she's living, I believe, happily ever after. I wish her the best.

Chapter Eleven

London. Judicial Punishment Training.

I had a nice little caning practice established after trooping up and down to London every month holding sessions at the Central London dungeon. A few of my clients had been saying that they would like to receive a Judicial Punishment.

Judicial Punishment is not for the faint-hearted. Caning is not for the faint-hearted. Judicial Punishment is on a higher, much higher level. It's a punishment that is still dealt out in Malaysia as severe punishment, and it's brutal. It is debatable that the punishments here are at the same level as a true judicial; I feel some people may *think* they are, and at the time they certainly may *feel* they are, and some people administering them may be stronger than others ... but realistically, I suspect they simply are not at the same level.

For whatever reason, a few people want to take things to the extreme. I suppose that's life, really. They want to climb the highest mountain; run the fastest race, or the furthest; walk around the world; sail around the world; experience a parachute free fall ... They want to do different things. Well, in its own way, Judicial Punishment is such an extreme activity. Very, very extreme!

Because I'd had a few people asking me, I decided to embark on a monthly, year long training regime to culminate into a full Judicial Punishment session. I had two people who wanted to train for it. One was Justin Stripes, a faithful follower of caning I've already spoken about in earlier chapters.

The other was a gentleman called Mark. He was in his late fifties and had been enjoying receiving the cane for some time now.

He used to drive down from Bedfordshire in his Rolls Royce (he owned a successful string of garages), park on the perimeter of London and jump on the tube to Warren Street to come and see me, pretty much every month. He also wanted to go that little bit further.

I developed a regime of practicing my caning and both of them getting used to it. Every month we'd go a little bit further; a little more strokes, a little bit heavier strokes, different canes, different levels of canes, meting out different levels of punishment.

I'd start out with a junior cane on one of them; a lot thinner, twangy and stingy. Then we would gradually progress through the thicknesses of weights of canes, until we got to judicial level.

I devised a training programme and stuck to it religiously. The programme usually comprised of administering an assortment of canes over each man. Estimating the percentage of force I'd use, I might use a Senior Rattan, fifty percent capability for one month, then maybe build it up to seventy-five percent the next month, then build up the number of strokes received from there.

Contrary to what some people think, a Judicial Punishment isn't about the number of strokes, so it isn't about taking one hundred strokes and that's the Judicial Punishment. When practiced, it's usually a number under twelve strokes; twelve probably being the maximum because of the force behind it. It is so forceful, twelve strokes at maximum force is all people can take.

But for my purposes, I was aiming to build up to about a hundred strokes on each individual in the practice sessions. I would do them in either batches of ten or twelve with different canes. I would lay the canes out in order of use, starting with the mildest first, and gradually building it up. And, of course, everybody enjoyed it … well, eventually!

'Enjoy' isn't the right word, actually! Everybody *endured* it! It was later on they got to enjoy it. The enjoyment is in the after-effects. That's when the endorphins kick-in – when the beating stops. And you wonder why? Why do people want to do this? Everyone has their reasons. Some are more complicated than others. For some, it's just the sheer determination of willpower to achieve it; it's an achievement to them. And my goodness me, it *is* an achievement! If you can withstand a Judicial Punishment ... wow! The adrenaline rush each participant gets out of this is incredible – me included! Win-win all the way.

Normally in BDSM there are 'safe words' agreed on between the Dominant and the submissive. The submissive uses these safe words whenever their tolerance level or boundaries are crossed. Believe it or not, it's actually the submissive who is always the one in control in the dynamic. The safe word I use is *Mercy* – I feel it's quite appropriate for the circumstances.

In our particular dynamic, however, the two people I was training didn't have safe words. I was so used to caning them without using any restraint that I didn't need a safe word, because I could tell by their body language. This is where professionalism and knowledge of craft comes into play.

Different people on different days have different levels of being able to accept the pain. I know it sounds really strange, but some days it really hurts and some days it doesn't really hurt ... as much. Obviously, it really hurts all the time. Even room temperature affects the level of pain. When its warmer/hot, well, you bleed easier. There are different levels of hurt.

For the purpose of the judicial training, we trained for eleven sessions; eleven monthly sessions, every single one of which both recipients attended. And then after that, it was all about the build-up to the actual Judicial Punishment Day.

I had previously arranged for a friend to film it. This friend was a film maker. He used to film a lot of sporting activities, and this was certainly a sporting activity type of film! I heard he used to edit them as well. I was very pleased about this. However, as often happens in these types of situations, people cry off.

For some people they just lose their nerve and it's as simple as that. This is a big thing, make no mistake about it. It's a big thing to undertake. But on this occasion, it was the actual filming guy who cried off! He actually told me, first thing on the morning of the shoot, that he couldn't come. I couldn't believe it! *What in the world?! On the day of the shoot! Unbelievable!* Apparently, he just wasn't up to it. Frustrating, to say the least! But we weren't about to let that thwart us, not while I was in charge! No way! It had taken a full year to build up to the big day. I wasn't going to let this ruin such a momentous occasion. I had to think fast!

As luck would have it, Justin Stripes was around first thing in the morning. Our Judicial Punishment was arranged for the afternoon, so I sent him off to go and buy a camcorder and a tripod. Dutifully, he came back with a super camcorder and tripod, perfectly suitable for filming the Judicial Punishment. Unfortunately, we just had to make do with the static filming, though, which is a shame. It was such short notice. We just had go with what we had. At least it was something after all that work we put in ... all that time and dedication ... all that training!

We held the Judicial Punishment punishment training and the actual Judicial Punishment in the dungeon in London. It was very central, close to a hospital; it made giving directions so much easier!

Madam A had a procession of bitchy Mistresses who knew little to nothing about being a Dominatrix. They just wanted easy money. None of them lasted. It was the dungeon keeper, *Madam A* herself, a traditional, high quality Old-School Mistress, who agreed to announce the sentencing and commit these 'misdemeanours' to Judicial Punishment under the hands of *Madam Rattan*.

Both 'defendants' took the punishment. It was very severe. For the punishment they were strapped down to the whipping bench. They took it, turn on turn. I gave them in batches of ten – six batches of ten, then built up to the final batch, which was delivered at full force! They both took it very well. And it was all filmed onto celluloid.

And afterwards? What does one do after a marathon of extreme proportions like that? We all went home for tea of course! Just like that. No blaze of glory, no shouting from the hilltops. These two men had achieved a personal goal, possibly one from their – very personal – bucket lists.

I never saw or heard from Mark again. *How strange,* I thought. But, on reflection, understanding more and more about how people think; the determination to achieve such a feat was probably on his bucket list, and he left on a high, having achieved the most severe punishment of all.

Chapter Twelve

Canary Wharf: Turn-Down Service, featuring Night of the Cane and Elation to Disappointment

As *Twisted Sisters* we had been going to London on a fairly regular basis, about once every six weeks or so. When we took the bookings, not everyone wanted Double-Domme sessions, but we always made sure we had a 'run' of sessions.

Usually I stayed at Kensington, but my contact, the friendly manager, had told me that there was a brand new hotel at Canary Wharf which was opening soon. Better still, he told me, they were doing 'trial-runs' for staff training and the room rates were exceptionally heavily discounted. So we thought we'd take up the offer and stay at Canary Wharf for a change.

The Canary Wharf hotel was very nice; real wood panelling and lovely rooms. This was a brand new hotel. It was rumoured that this chain of hotels allowed a £75,000 budget per room when building, so you can imagine the quality. Canary Wharf is a fairly affluent area, situated in the Isle of Dogs, close to South Quay footbridge, which connects to the centre of Canary Wharf. Part of the regeneration of London, it's considered to be the secondary business area of London and is clearly visible when flying into Heathrow or City Airport – probably even Gatwick Airport as well!

The rooms were brand new, pristine and lavishly furnished with dark wooden furniture, sumptuous rich velvet curtains and throws, with soft, thick carpet; built to last. Quality was paramount. The artwork in the rooms were prints of London, and some of the rooms had the most glorious views of the docks which connected to the Thames.

The Executive Lounge was one of the best I have experienced. It was superb! Its special hors d'oeuvre served around six o'clock every evening, better than any dinner; canapés followed by a cool refreshing, relaxing drink … delicious; coffee and biscuits during the day; or a lovely afternoon tea with sandwiches and mini cakes, all freshly made and brought up to the exec lounge and laid out in the buffet area for people to help themselves to their favourite delicate sandwiches, pastries and cakes. Quiet, peaceful, with a gorgeous view overlooking the Thames; life just doesn't get any better than this!

I used to take my subs to the Executive Lounge. It used to make them squirm and put them on edge a little bit before their session. A waiting game. I'd have them get me bone china cups of tea or coffee, or afternoon tea if their session coincided. Canary Wharf afternoon tea is delectably sumptuous.

The lounge itself was on a higher floor with a glorious view of the Thames. It was divine to relax with my paper and a coffee, watching the world drift by on the Thames. I could sit and watch barges, speedboats, and the like sail up and down the river from there.

And I remember the breakfasts. Most hotels do a great breakfast but oh, this went up a notch! They even served freshly juiced wheatgrass! And sushi for Japanese guests, who were often frequenting the hotel. Not sure why they stayed in this particular part of London; maybe they had something to do with the financial district.

The hotel, I discovered, even had a turn-down service with the beds at night, which I didn't realise until it was too late. We'd gone out for a meal, came back and found the bedding turned down and a chocolate on the pillow! I'd left all my whips, my leather and suede floggers, and long, handmade leather gloves on the bed!

I always have a little laugh to myself about that. I don't know what the chambermaid must've thought! Probably cheered her up; a bit of fun to gossip over with other staff when she took her break. I'm sure hotel staff have seen and heard it all before!

One thing about me was I always invested in quality. Everything I had, all my equipment, was top quality, because I always ensured they were purchased from a top quality leather/cane manufacturer called *'Quality Control'* based near Birmingham. I always chose red and black designs, and the canes were a quality second to none. These were my preference.

Canary Wharf is quite close to the East End of London and, at that time, had a couple of BDSM clubs in that quarter. There was also a dungeon there that I was keen to check out, but when I got to see it, it just wasn't suitable. I think the owner sold it soon after I'd looked at it, because I never got to use it.

Anyway, on this particular trip I was on my own, and my room actually overlooked the Thames. It was amazing. I had been upgraded from a room to a suite! It was huge, luxurious and oh so quiet. I didn't want to leave! I also had the most beautiful view, though I don't know which bit of the Thames it overlooked. I just enjoyed that aspect of the Thames where it curved round and meandered along its merry way.

I was at the Canary Wharf because I had a client, a Master who liked giving corporal punishment (CP) to his submissives and who thought that, in the spirit of being a good and learned Master, he should experience what he was subjecting his submissives to, which is very considerate and very fair in my book. Really good. So he'd booked me for a caning session.

On arrival, I checked him out. Looking maybe in his forties or fifties, he was quite fit. Actually, he was very, very fit! White, Calvin Klein boxer shorts ... *oh* ... and really well-toned. I gave him twelve strokes of the cane while he leant over the window ledge overlooking the Thames. *How amusing, I thought, here he is, ultra-fit, butt naked, being caned by me overlooking the Thames, as the boats sail their way up and down the river.* Did he wave at them passing? I'm not sure. I can't remember. But oh boy, that was fun!

We kept in contact for quite a while. He took me out for dinner in a lovely restaurant in Kensington the next time I came down to London. He was a nice guy, and it was good for him to experience what he subjected his submissives to. He worked for a firm of stockbrokers, though I can't remember where. He was in charge of security, probably something to do with cybersecurity ... not that I know. It's none of my business.

Enjoying our dinner date over a decent bottle of wine, we got to know each other a little better. He was a London lad, born and bred; brash, ballsy, and quite enigmatic. During the course of the evening, he let it slip he was well-endowed ... nine inches!

Well! Up to that point I had never seen one that size, so thought, *This I've got to see!* So, in the taxi on the way back to my hotel before dropping me off, I asked him if he wanted to pop in for a coffee. Unfortunately, the Executive Lounge had just closed, so he *had* to come up to my suite ... enough said! Safe to say, he hadn't exaggerated!

I went to my first '*Night of the Cane*' event while staying at Canary Wharf. Justin Stripes came and picked me up in his Jaguar and drove us. I think he got completely lost, but it didn't matter; it was a good night out. I wore my lovely black velvet cape with bright red silk lining to go to the venue. It covered my fetish wear nicely without drawing too much attention while leaving the hotel ... under the radar.

Night of the Cane ended up being one of my favourite events. It was a competition you entered and the Mistresses or Masters competing gave six strokes of the cane, ideally but not essentially in a five bar gate pattern, judged on Style, Power and Accuracy. If you drew blood, you were automatically disqualified. Blood must not be drawn. I recall it was mainly Mistresses that entered, but there were a few Masters; not many, but a few.

The first time I went, it was held in a wonderful old Victorian building in Hackney. It had a huge stage, and everything was built with wood, though I believe the building was demolished soon after. In East London, the venue was teeming with a diverse, eclectic, and interesting mix of people. Some entrants were very theatrical about it, while some just did a very 'workmanlike' job of people's bottoms! You can be workmanlike and still have a certain style, and that was me; I wasn't as theatrical as some, but I had power & accuracy. Ah, it was a great event.

At the time, *Night of the Cane* was run by Ishmael Skyes. We got to know each other very slowly and carefully. He was not everyone's cup of tea; just like me, really. But he did trust me ... eventually, I think!

Night of the Cane is a legendary event, it was fun and bought out my competitive streak a little, though winning didn't really matter, it was the atmosphere on the night; it was electric, edgy, mesmerising and enthralling, all wrapped up in an event I hold dear.

He was heavily involved in the old website called *Informed Consent* and ran regular events including a legendary Burns night, and a Boat Cruise *aka 'The Boat'* on the Thames which again, was, and still is, legendary! The stories of people being tied to the mast and flogged in full view of people walking alongside the Thames!

I think he lost his venue in the end. Venues were very difficult to come by then. Some people didn't want to risk the papers turning up and stuff like that, so it was quite tricky to make a success of any type of BDSM venue.

Anyway, that night, a couple were playing the part of 'Lady Penelope' and 'Parker', her driver, in the competition. They were completely theatrical about it. She came in smoking a cigarette, saying, "Parker? Parker!"

"Yes M'Lady?"

Well! It just captured my imagination, and I thought, *I wanna do that! I wanna enter!*

I only entered a couple of times. Once I entered the competition when it was held in an old pub basement near Kings Cross. The basement was really, really hot. Difficult conditions to cane bottoms, because when they get really warm, they bleed easily. Half of the candidates, including me, ended up getting disqualified after drawing blood from only three or four strokes of the cane, which was a real shame. But who cares, just being there was a buzz!

Although I do remember that year's events with frustration for another reason as well!

My faithful sub, steve, had driven me down to London. His birthday was looming and that evening I had been chatting to a Mistress friend who epitomised everything he loved and worshipped in a Mistress. She was beautiful, voluptuous, a woman of colour, his ideal. I hatched a plan to give him an early birthday present on the Sunday before we returned up north. She was aware our schedule was tight and promised me to give him a session first thing in the morning, before we began our drive back up North.

After *Night of the Cane*, the next morning, I sent him off on an errand to her premises. He was *so* excited! Unfortunately, she failed to even answer the door! He waited and waited and knocked and knocked … but to no avail. He contacted me in a panic, not knowing what to do; my desperate calls to her went unanswered. She was a no show! Such disappointment! She eventually wrote and apologised a few days later and said he could come over the next Sunday.

Didn't she get that we lived hundreds of miles away?! Typical of a Mistress to think the world revolved around her and her timetable!

What got me was she had made an arrangement with a fellow Mistress and then broke her word, again! That's not how things are done in this lifestyle. I never contacted her again. I won't write her name here, but I have heard this same story a few times. A loose cannon. So fickle! So unreliable! So dishonest! Playing with people's fantasies and making promises that are not kept. That is not respectful.

In my world you just don't do that. My contempt for her is high. My disappointment for steve was great. I was seething for days! Not just for steve, but for the contempt with which she treated a promise! So unprofessional! It made a mockery of the whole profession.

Thankfully, there aren't many people I've come across like her. In fact, no-one else. As I said, a loose cannon. The whole scene is based on honesty and respect. People like that don't stop me from doing what interests me though. The incident wasn't about the lifestyle, it was about her un-professionalism.

The next time I went back to *Night of the Cane* it ended in triumph and my claim to fame. I came second in the competition! I was runner-up with *Miss Hastings-Gore*, who is quite a theatrical lady, very experienced and well-known on the scene. She's still around on the scene today; hosting Saturday School, amongst other things. What a night! It was a great night all round. I loved it, and such a great way to catch up with the other Mistresses.

All-in-all, I think I might have gone about three times. And then I think … oh yes … and then I bought the club I run today and wasn't able to get away on Saturdays. *Night of the Cane*, for me anyway, is legendary and is going.

Chapter Thirteen

London: Twisted Sisters;
Fire Alarm During Session

As *Twisted Sisters*, we didn't go down to London all the time, just when we had enough bookings, so on this particular trip, it made it worth our while for us to both go down.

We started off with a two-hour booking with a cross-dresser who basically wanted us to help him put on a dress, do his make-up and hair, very carefully put him in stockings and heels, then he became a she and wanted to strut around in the hotel room like a slut. This is quite common with crossdressers. Once they get their wig, make-up, dress & heels on, because it's such a drastic change and once they realise that they can't be identified, they take on a completely different persona. They are transformed. It's definitely escapism for some.

This is often when the outrageous behaviour comes out. Not always, but sometimes they go to extremes in behaviour. And often, those extremes become very slutty. There are some, however, who dress up just to get in touch with their feminine side. My interpretation is that crossdressers (CD) like to dress up to have an alter ego and do outrageous things. Transvestites (TVs) go a step further; they may be exploring their finer feelings a little or a lot more.

Some are considering going further, and by that, I mean transgender. Not many people rush into such a big change; not many have the nerve, courage, confidence, or support. This journey is not one that is taken lightly. Expectations on men (it's not only men, but it's only men that I have experience with) can last a lifetime, and often people can get to their 50s before they have the courage to make a change. This journey is a difficult one, people's reaction is not always as it should be; though things are improving, it is still often a bumpy road to travel.

Some men have very masculine jobs. It must be quite lonely to have be so alpha male, to always have to show how clever they are; how capable they are; how masculine they are ... they miss a certain softness in their lives. Some men have very pressurised jobs and for some this is like letting off steam, similar to the way a pressure cooker does. They want a bit of femininity. They want to wear nice clothes. It helps balance their lives. Of course, most CDs – virtually every single CD I know – have got fantastic legs and no cellulite. They look wonderful if they can master the art of tottering around in high heels.

Anyway, the first hour of this two-hour appointment had been spent getting our client all ready and dressed up for the complete look: make-up, hair, clothes, stockings, high heels ... and just as she was about to start strutting around, the fire alarm went off. And it wasn't a test! Oh my goodness me!

The sheer panic! The three of us just looked at each other. What do we do? Do we leave the room dressed like this? I mean, it was very exciting for the TV, who'd only ever, ever dressed in private before. The thought of being forced to leave the room and go and stand at the Fire Assembly Point outside! Oh my lord! Totally incognito! Totally unrecognisable for sure! It turned out to be a quite tempting part of the dilemma for her. For us though, it was something entirely different. *What? Being exposed in these outfits!* OMG! It wouldn't be helping us keep under the radar, that's for sure!

Sensibly I had my thinking head on, so *Mistress Torture* – that's me as one of the *Twisted Sisters* – rang down to Reception to check if it was a test alarm. We didn't think it was because we hadn't been told about it. *What was happening?!* Thankfully they told us that the fire alarm was a false alarm, and we didn't have to evacuate the building. Phew!

But what excitement! The TV preened and strutted around the room, even venturing out and tottering up and down the corridor! That was quite brave. You don't know who she might have run into! That, of course, was all part of the fun, and the adrenaline rush she got from doing that was off the scale!

Also on this trip, we saw a young Italian lad – Lets call him Joe, probably in his thirties, used to come over from Italy and see me every three months. His fetish was grovelling at my feet, worshipping my feet, and being spanked. On this day, he decided he wanted a Double-Domme session, so we duly had him crawl across the floor to each of us. We sat in different places across the hotel room and had him crawling everywhere we directed.

He liked to be humiliated. He liked to be laughed at. We enjoyed that for a little while, then we decided we were going to spank him. And *Mistress Torment* was going to spank him first.

I ordered him to bend over her knee, to go *'over the knee'* (OTK) and be prepared to be spanked. With that I went into the bathroom to wash my hands and on return, instead of bending over *Mistress Torment's* knee, he was actually sat on her lap with his back to her front, sitting like a baby as if he were about to be bounced up and down on her knee! It's one of those things that you just had to be there to appreciate.

Lord! Imagine! Walking out of the bathroom and seeing him sat the wrong way! It was so funny! And the look on *Mistress Torment's* face – she was gobsmacked! She didn't know what to do! I just looked and burst out laughing. I had to go back into the bathroom, I was laughing so hard. And I couldn't stop! I really didn't want to laugh so heartily in front of him, but it had been so funny! Especially during a session like this, where there's quite a lot of excitement and adrenaline floating around – even more so when *Mistress Torment* and I do our sessions. We just bounce off each other.

I was in absolute, almost uncontrollable laughter! Hiding in the bathroom I had to stuff a towel in my mouth to try and stop the raucous laughter. It's one thing laughing at somebody to humiliate them, but this laughter ... well, it wasn't very professional, really, so I had to stop myself. Oh dear! That was so funny! That was a very memorable trip indeed!

While still on the same trip, we also had a session with somebody who used to call himself *My Naughty Nephew*. He was a very naughty boy. He used to get up to all sorts of pranks. He used to have to come to me for chastisement and would have to confess to all the little pranks he got up to.

Before he arrived, I would line up all the canes in order of use and lie them all on the top of the bed. He would be ordered to bend over the bottom of the bed, so he was forced to look at the canes, knowing exactly which ones were going to be used.

I always started to warm him up with a good spanking first. He was quite a little squirmer. He just couldn't keep still! Then we used to work our way through the canes. There was usually about ten; sometimes there was a birch as well, and sometimes a Tawse. I would give him ten or twelve strokes of every cane, birch, and Tawse; whatever was at hand at the time.

Of course, every person had to count whenever I was caning them, so I didn't lose track. And if anyone counted wrong, we had to go right back to the beginning and start all over again! *My Naughty Nephew* was a very pleasant distraction. What a lovely man.

Another submissive I knew, a real famous celebrity look-alike, had invited me several times to his home whenever I was in London. He was an Air Traffic Controller and always wore a certain aftershave. He looked and smelled delicious.

When *Mistress Torment* returned home, I finally agreed and made the trip down to Hampshire to visit him and stayed at his apartment. My friend *Lady Susan* lived in the same area, so when I went to stay with him, I invited her over.

All he wanted to do was give women oral sex. She came over, he cooked a meal for us all in his apartment, then afterwards, over coffee and drinks, I sat on the sofa chatting to her while she sat on his face as he pleasured her! We had such an enjoyable evening. What more could a woman want? Good company, good conversation, glass of wine in hand, just as any perfectly normal evening should be!

Chapter Fourteen

Bondage Without Restraint and Twisted Sisters Fun

These are my own interpretations, explanations, and rationalisations of certain situations within the BDSM scene. I am not the expert, and I'm sure other people will have different interpretations and definitions of part, all, and/or any of this.

Sadomasochism is where people interpret pain as pleasure. The sadomasochism power exchange (PE) is about opening aspects of people that are deep and hidden. Undisclosed and undiscovered fantasies are not just sexual, although they do tend to have a sexual leaning. These psychological and sexual aspects of communication are explored in ways that are very different from day-to-day interactions. People escape themselves to meet themselves. And when they do, they simultaneously lose control, yet gain control of something much deeper inside of themselves.

I had a lot of fun unearthing and discovering this side of people's 'hidden traits'. I was quite tuned into people's body language, and I understood people, which probably made me quite unique in that respect – not everybody does. For some it's all about being sadistic and applying pain, which is fine for them, I guess.

I tend to use other means than restraint to secure people when delivering punishment. I'm not really interested in tying people up with ropes, nor any other form of restraint such as leather straps, handcuffs, that sort of thing. I'm more interested in bondage without restraint.

Bondage without restraint is the code I prefer to adopt, not always, but most of the time. This means I get to use the recipient sub's mind and willpower to make them stay in position of their own accord, thus making the sub a co-conspirator with everything that goes on. Win-win; that's what it's all about. Win-win is one of my mantras.

For example, during a session, I'd have two different positions: Position One and Position Two. Whichever one the sub chose, he would have to stay in that position.

In Position One, I spank, flog, cane, whatever the session is about until the sub can bear it no more, and then they move. it's their way of telling me enough is enough.

When they've had a rest and are ready to resume, then they re-assume the position. If a sub decides that they're ready for more – more strokes of the cane, more torture, more humiliation – then they put themselves in Position Two, knowing full well there is more to come. This ensures no ties that bind, other than their own free will and agreement.

As *Twisted Sisters,* our Double-Domme persona, we did all sorts of things, including deciding to specialise in providing a fantasy kidnap. It was one of the most popular fantasy scenarios at the time, for both men and women. Having somebody's kidnap fantasy fulfilled – being an unwilling captive; a sex slave; naughty boys and girls removed, degraded, disciplined, restrained, and caned; caged and treated like a dog; or kept prisoner and interrogated until a 'secret' was divulged ... the list goes on. Kidnap was on a lot of people's fantasy lists.

The fantasy kidnap could last anything from twelve hours to twelve days. It was expensive. It was a psychologically stimulating and memorable experience. Only fit and healthy captives could apply, and we did have a few of those.

In one such scenario we actually lifted somebody from Sainsbury's car park early one Saturday morning. It was thrilling! Thrilling for us all, I must say!

One of our other specialities was organising weekends away for submissives who wanted a little bit more than a one-hour session – maybe they were thinking about delving more into the lifestyle. This type of lifestyle can be very consuming. Not only did we provide this service as *Twisted Sisters*, we also went out on our own with this as well.

When we organised a weekend away, we used to cater for two or three subs at a time. One of them arranged the transport, one of them arranged the accommodation, and the other arranged the food and drink, so the cost of the weekend turned out to be quite reasonable. Of course, we arranged the timetable and itinerary. And all the subs were instructed to buy a gift to present to each Mistress at the end of the weekend.

Typically, the timetable ran like this: on a Friday evening we, or I, would arrive. One of the subs would have already arrived, to check-in, check the accommodation over, prepare the room, and to greet the Mistress; always ensuring that the Mistresses had a drink on arrival, that they were comfortable, and unpacking their luggage for them.

Then the second sub would arrive, followed by the third. One aspect that was very important was the subs' inspection. The subs would stand naked in front of the Mistress and the Mistress would check them; rubbing their hands over their nipples, perhaps, tickling their cock and balls, bending them over slightly to spank them. These subs could be both male and female, by the way.

At that point their medical history would be checked. For all my sessions I always checked their medical history. **"Are there any medical conditions I need to be aware of?"** Very important! And, as long as everybody passed, the weekend would continue.

We'd have a ceremonial ritual of dressing the subs. Generally, this would be a collar and loin cloth, or some such item of appropriate clothing. Then we'd be entertained by the subs with a short play or a showcase of their artistic and/or creative talents and skills; some sang, some danced, played the guitar, read poems ... whatever the sub decided to show us, followed by dinner. One of the submissives prepared dinner, one perhaps played the role of butler, while another attended to our needs, possibly by giving us a foot massage or pedicure.

At dinner, some of the subs were allowed to eat with us while, depending on their levels of interest, others may have eaten separately, or eaten from dog bowls. We'd finish dinner with coffee and mints or perhaps a nice Irish Coffee, something like that.

After dinner we often played board games throughout the evening and the winner would help us bathe and prepare for bed. The winner could also have the privilege to sleep outside Mistresses' door, or possibly at the bottom of their bed if they had been particularly good, in case they needed anything through the night, while attached to possibly a lead or maybe a remote control of sorts.

The weekend would continue, always with a brisk walk and generally with some form of humiliation outdoors to make us chuckle and to make them squirm. Instructions such as getting one of the subs to hop along the road, or I would have them climb into the middle of a bush for a plant cutting, or up a tree; or carry my handbag; just little quirky things, the list is endless. We'd probably then continue to the coffee shop in a vanilla environment, whereby no submissive traits were visibly shown, such as carrying my coffee on a tray, paying for the coffees. ... Of course, we knew otherwise. There were always underlying threats going on.

We'd generally have play in the afternoon before the subs prepared dinner and cocktails. After that we'd perhaps hold a pain threshold competition. It was just a lovely, relaxed weekend of decadence, immersing themselves in everything they had fantasised about, whether that be physical pain, humiliation, or just serving. A myriad of different things that different people liked.

One of my submissives who came for one such weekend had, as part of showcasing his 'talent', came up with the words to Barry Manilow's song *Copacabana* ... with twist!

"Her name was Susan, she was a Mistress,
Flower in her hair, she could kill you with a stare,
She had a bull whip and did the cha-cha,
Andrew was her slave, she would take him to his grave,
She'd tie him to a wall, then kick him in the balls,
Whip him black and blue and he begged for more.

At the dungeon, Dominate dungeon
The hottest spot this side of London
At the dungeon, Dominate dungeon
Music and thrashing were always in fashion
At the dungeon, Dominate dungeon.

His name was shitface, he was a loser,
Crawled across the floor, his knees were rather sore
Then he saw Mistress, he had a hard on
He loved her rounded arse, she was a different class
Andrew leapt from the wall, they scuffled on the floor
Mistress cracked her whip and they knew, the, score.

At the dungeon, Dominate dungeon
The hottest spot this side of London
At the dungeon, Dominate dungeon
Music and thrashing were always in fashion
At the dungeon, Dominate dungeon.

Her name is Susan, she is a Mistress
That was thirty years ago, but she still runs the show,
She still owns Steve, and still owns shitface,
Doesn't let them talk, she takes them for a walk,
She sits there so refined,
She can torment your mind,
Still loves to use the cane on her slut's behind,

At the dungeon, Dominate dungeon
The hottest spot this side of London
At the dungeon, Dominate dungeon
Music and thrashing were always in fashion
At the dungeon, Dominate dungeon."

You can see that it's not all just about being serious. We had some great fun! Having fun was my interpretation. It wasn't everybody's way of looking at it, but it was my way; so it was the right way.

Everyone is right in this lifestyle, when you're working out what you like and what you don't like. There are things you should and shouldn't do and there are protocols that you should and shouldn't follow. You'd be frowned upon if you don't follow certain protocols.

I did have an unusual request once, and repeated a few times by the same person. One day I received a phone call. The person calling had an Asian accent. He requested that he come for a humiliation session with me. I asked for a bit more information of what he wanted, and he requested that I racially abuse him. I was speechless! *What?! You've got to be kidding!* I thought in total shock! *No way!* Needless to say, I didn't accept the booking the first time, nor his consecutive requests a good while later. I just could *not* do it!

Still to this day I can't understand why someone would want this. But then, on reflection, I realise nothing surprises me. What is wrong in some people's eyes is the salve to another, who searches to soothe their troubled or restless minds.

Having said all that, your way is the right way, and you will most likely find somebody, should you be so inclined, who you can meet to fulfil your fantasy without being belittled, or humiliated, or thought differently of. And that's very liberating. Very liberating indeed.

Chapter Fifteen

London: Barnet Bastille
and the Caning Courts

I had a particular interest in caning. I enjoyed it, and I was very good at it. You tend to enjoy the things that you're good at, so I ended up specialising in caning … hence the name 'Madam Rattan'. It was my passion. I don't know why. Perhaps it was because I could vent my feelings about previous events in my life? But it only worked for me if it was a win-win situation. Had I been a true sadist, this wouldn't have mattered.

It took a long time to come up with the name 'Madam Rattan'. I think that the name is one of the most important parts of everything; in business names, event names, Mistress names. If it does what it says on the tin, all the better. If its catchy and memorable – perfect!

Rattan. The reason I called myself Madam Rattan is because Rattan is a type of cane; exceptionally strong, durable, and versatile, yet it can absorb more impact than hardwood. That's because it's not as heavy as hardwood, which tends to transfer the impact into the body. Rattan is traditionally grown, is easily available – makes it easier to train with – and reduces injuries. Ideal for training purposes.

Accurate. Hard. Soft. Each stroke I administered was determined by my understanding of people's wants and needs and what aspect of corporal punishment (CP) they particularly enjoyed.

As people mature, they tend to look back and reflect on things that happened to them when they were younger, relying on them to give them some sort of solid base and stability forged from fond or consistent memories. It seemed to provide some sort of framework to help structure and shape their lives.

For a lot of people CP reflected a time when they had maybe been to a boarding school, and had endured punishments administered to them for whatever reason.

I'm not saying that's why everybody does it, not by any means, but to some people that is why they feel the need for it. They want to revert back to a time in their lives where they felt that they were cared for, nurtured in whatever form they experienced at a pivotal time in their lives. Nurturing can come in lots of different forms.

I had a few regular, loyal people that used to come to me on my regular monthly jaunts to London. People that, due to their situation and or position in life, only had a limited amount of time they could afford, who would pop out from work, have an hour's caning, and then go back to work again, sitting on their sore bottoms, reliving their caning experience while they were on a high!

Every time they move, they are reminded of the session. In time, the welts on their skin disappear, to be replaced by bruises, reminding them all over again. Some people wear their lines or bruises with pride. People such as athletes, or people with partners, for example, don't want, under *any* circumstances, to have marks that show. Can you imagine elite athletes going to training and showing their marks in the showers afterwards? To counteract this, many Mistresses use a wet, wrung out towel to cane through. It's not a guaranteed science, but it does help.

Being caned releases lots of feel-good endorphins. A lot of people get a great sense of achievement from undergoing and enduring a caning session. The cane really hurts. It's not everybody's cup of tea; it takes a particular sort of person.

I often used to think, based on the first couple of strokes, *You're not possibly up to this ... can you take it? No. It's just not possible. You're not gonna last the session.* But they do! And the euphoria they feel for having lasted through that session is amazing. That can give both of us a high for quite a while.

The recipient certainly has a high, but people don't realise that the dominant gets a high as well, and to varying degrees. Sadists may be sexually excited by it. Some Dominants will simply enjoy the feeling of a job well done in the fact of the recipient being happy and their needs being met. Win-win.

Conversely, the drop afterwards isn't as good, and that too is felt in varying degrees. After an adrenaline high comes a drop. You may feel it quickly, or it may hit you the next day or the day after, which can make you feel low, tired and/or quiet. For me, I just need to zone out, watch daft television, eat rubbishy foods and stay warm. It soon passes.

That's not the only reason people want to be chastised. I know somebody in particular that did something in his very younger days that, though a minor incident, is one he bitterly regretted. It had a dramatic effect on him and receiving the cane was his penance for it. I relate this type of reasoning to those religious people that beat themselves. It's a sort of analogue to that.

I had a few people that I had more than an hour's relationship with. We were firm friends … and through our friendship, an idea hatched. That idea was to hold judicial punishment or corporal punishment sessions.

At that time, I worked in a printers' and, uncannily, that printers' had been given a job of printing a Magistrates Court Guide. What timing! So, I adapted the guidance to be just like a Magistrates Court. I wrote out all the guidance pages; literally pages and pages and pages of it! And I had the Law Books. I had all the ingredients for a court session! Perfect!

We started the Magistrates Court sessions at the hotel where I had equipped my dungeon. We took over the bar area on the ground floor on a Saturday afternoon, raised the floor behind the bar with pallets, and installed three magistrates' seats, one of which was my throne I'd brought up from the dungeon.

The three magistrates were other Mistresses. We had a Clerk of Court; a Prosecuting Barrister; a Defending Barrister; witnesses …

The 'defendants' that were being 'heard' in court had previously been notified of what their offence was. It was all written down. And they got their case heard, complete with witnesses and a gallery of onlookers!

We went through the whole scenario of 'trying' each individual's case. It was all done 'tongue in cheek', of course. Some of the offences were just plain silly and most were improbable, though some seemed quite realistic. That just added to the fun. The recipients got to write their own defence. In some cases, the recipients were even allowed to write their own offences! Making a jail break, blackmailing someone, stealing cars, crazy, unbelievable situations ... that sort of thing.

The Court would adjourn for a little buffet lunch before commencing the sentencing. Of course, everybody was found guilty! Each received varying degrees of punishment, administered in order of severity, though the level of severity of the Judicial Cane and the American Strap is debatable. They are both highly effective.

Punishments were always strokes of the cane. How many strokes of which canes I used would depend on their level of experience; it could also include the Birch, the Senior Rattan, the Lochgelly Tawse and the Junior Rattan.

All guilty persons were marched upstairs from the dungeon. One of the defendants had an old 'chain gang' handcuff set, so we chained every 'offender' together and they all had to march in unison, come upstairs and receive their punishment one by one while the remainder stood there, awaiting their 'fate'. The anticipation was incredible! Once or twice, we lined everybody up after their punishments and took photographs of all their bottoms!

Of course, these Court sessions didn't exactly follow the letter of the law, but they were very good; very close to it. They became very popular and were very good fun, so much so that at the end of the session we used to get six or seven of the witnesses or those in the gallery applying to go to court! It was always a really good day. A triumph! And so funny!

You'd probably have had to be there at the time to appreciate the atmosphere. The rowdiness! The cheers! The derogatory comments from the onlookers in the gallery; whistling and jeering! It was just like holding a Court session from the olden days! The Judge had to call "Order!" several times throughout the trial. What a laugh! What fun! Everyone there was involved.

We had quite a few Court sessions, about five or six, as I recall. Such was its popularity, we thought, *Right! Let's take it to London!*

Finding the right place was quite difficult, but we achieved our aim. One of the first places we held it was at a place called the *Barnet Bastille*.

Unlike the imagery of the name, it was some sort of unit on a very small modern industrial estate. We had to walk past the garage, where the mechanics knew exactly where we were going! That was a bit uncomfortable. It was a long way from the centre of London; a good thirty-minute ride in the taxi on a good day, providing there was not too much traffic.

It wasn't really the right place, but we held one of the sessions there anyway; there was plenty of space there, a bonus for London. We also got to hold a session in the dungeon I used to use in Central London. As you can imagine, dungeons weren't two-a-penny, even in London! Not for what we were using them for, anyway; and they weren't easy to find either! Even now I don't think there are more than half a dozen.

Because it was all very theatrical, it generally turned out as a nice, fun event. Oh, and just to add to the theatrics of it all, whenever I went down London, I used to have a medical professional with me. At these particular sessions, I had my friend Raych, or sometimes Gracie. Both were medical professionals and performed medical checks on each defendant – essential for ensuring everybody was okay; whether they had any underlying health conditions, or were on medication, and if there was anything we needed be aware of.

In Judicial Corporal Punishment, there have been lots of cases of people collapsing due to diabetes/dehydration/adrenaline overload. Fortunately, this has only happened to me once, and once was enough.

Naturally we did all these very important and necessary checks! Raych would check them out and then she helped me with the Court and the sentencing ... we went the full nine yards!

However, she didn't like to watch the sentencing being carried out, so she would leave just before the end.

On one particular day we held our Court session, a central London venue, Raych left as usual. We completed the sentencing and, as was customary at the end of each session, we left the building one at a time, as there were a few of us in the dungeon and we didn't want to bring too much attention to ourselves and look conspicuous.

Anyway, on this particular day, as we were about to leave the dungeon, I heard an unusual sound … a helicopter buzzing around! You may not think that so strange, but in Central London, it was strange! It's not a flight path. Unless you're right under the flight path in Kensington, you don't hear anything in the air.

I dismissed the thought and didn't think anything more of it. That is until Raych sent a message to say, "The street has been cordoned off and there's a roadblock at each end of the street!" Well, you can imagine what was going through my head! My imagination went into overdrive! *Have the police found out that we were holding this judicial, magistrates court session and they were going to do a police raid any minute?!* I must admit I was more than a little bit nervous! We obviously couldn't stay there. The court event had finished so we all gradually left, one by one. I was always the last to leave.

The street was definitely closed off! It had been cordoned off with tape, flanked with police at each end, plus police vans were parked across the road!

I walked up to the cordoned area to meet Raych in the café, as planned, to have a cup of coffee and review the proceedings of the session and there she was, having a cup of coffee with the BBC News Team! Thankfully, I discovered, not for interrogation purposes; they were explaining what had happened and why the road was cordoned off.

Apparently, this guy had gone into the DVLA office, just around the corner from the dungeon, and held the place up! He had held people hostage and thrown a couple of computers out the window! I think he did it because he couldn't get his HGV licence test fee refunded or something. This was in April 2012. It was all over the news.

You may think that would be the end of it, but no. We caught a taxi to the station, then realised that there was a police van following us! Police were taking him from the DVLA offices where he'd being holding the hostages direct to the Magistrates Court! *Whoa!* For a moment I thought they were tailing us! What a very, very bizarre day!

Usually after the Magistrates session in London, we would retire to the local pub to have a drink and have a bit of a laugh and a chat because, you know, it was quite euphoric doing these Court sessions. Especially for the recipients! These sessions are not for everybody!

I never got to know who any of the participants were. I was paid to do it, but I didn't necessarily need to know who they were. I never did an ID check or anything like that. All I did was look them up via the website under the 'Corporal Punishment' section of the site(s) to contact these people via their alias/alter ego name. This was also an enjoyable pastime of mine. I found people to be quite trustworthy and they usually turned up, which isn't the case for all the sessions.

As I say, I didn't know who all these people were. All I knew was the name they gave me. And it was quite bizarre, because eighteen months later I was watching a TV programme, or the news or something like that, and lo and behold, there was this gentleman on television and I thought, *I know your face. And I know your bottom!* A Peer of the Realm, no less! I think that's what they call a Lord.

So yes, that was quite funny. And that was the Magistrates Court; a lot of fun. Yes, a lot of fun was had by all with that experience.

Chapter Sixteen

New York: First Trip

I'd set myself up a nice little business travelling around the UK to varying cities. I always enjoy travelling and staying in quality hotels, and staying in hotels on a regular basis was my bit of luxury that started from my childhood.

My parents didn't have much money and could only afford to take us camping every so often, so usually we just went for walks and picnics, which I loved. One day, they spotted a special offer for a two-night break in a then well known hotel chain. You could book anywhere within the UK with dinner, bed and breakfast included for a reasonable price, but best of all, *children went free!* I loved those occasional weekends away. So here I am, reliving parts of my childhood that I loved. See how easy it is?

One of my submissives, Patrick, the cross-dresser who I'd met at Lytham and who worked in New York regularly, had said to me previously, "You really should go to New York, Mistress. They would love you there. Caning, spanking and your English accent, you would go down a storm. You really should go. A real English Rose … they will love that, and they will love you."

I pondered over it for a little while, then thought, *I've never been to New York. In fact, have I even been to America? No, I don't think I have,* so I thought, *Why not! Let's do it!*

For the first visit, part of the fun and enjoyment was deciding where I was going to stay, along with all the travel plans associated with it. I love planning and organising things. I spent ages trying to locate and decide which hotel to book in New York. How ironic! Which hotel would you like to stay in? What a beautiful dilemma. Amazing!

They were all roughly around the same sort of price; then I discovered there was one at an address called 'Church Street'. *That's a good omen,* I thought, because I used to live on Church Street, where I owned a fish and chip shop in Devon. It was a no-brainer; it had my name on it. That's where I decided to stay.

That was just about all I had to go on. I didn't really know any more than that. I didn't understand the way New York was at all! But I knew the hotel was fairly central.

I'd booked a flight on British Airways, of course. I tried to use them whenever possible. My brother used to work for them, but apart from that, British Airways are British Airways are British Airways.! They had a good standard at the time.

Once I'd decided I was going to try my luck in New York, I started doing my research and discovered that there was a website in the US called *Eros*, which may still be around today. You could advertise there as a travelling Mistress. It was mainly an escort site, but there was also a section for BDSM; Dominatrix, that sort of thing. I remember you could advertise for a two-week stint for something like $35. It was crazy! It was great! I put out an advertisement that I was coming over. It was all very exciting!

I flew over and took Steve, my submissive with me. We flew into JFK Airport and arrived at night, as is the norm when arriving in New York, then took a yellow cab to the hotel. There was a fixed cost of no more than $60 for the taxi fare. We were excited ... we tried to chat to the taxi driver, but he was miserable! He spent most of the journey on his phone moaning, probably because it was a fixed fare and wasn't making anything extra out of it. His manner wasn't what we were expecting ... oh dear ...

I hadn't known whereabouts it was, but the hotel was right next to *Ground Zero*; a complete surprise to me. They'd put me in a room on something like the 56th floor! When I got in the lift, it was the fastest lift I've ever been in.

The room was beautiful. It had the most enormous picture window overlooking Brooklyn Bridge. A fantastic view; I mean, New York *is* a fantastic place. Breakfast was included with the deal and the breakfast area overlooked *Ground Zero*. That was an amazing place. Such an ethereal feeling. So poignant. They were still knocking everything down at that point. Such sadness.

When 9/11 happened ... I don't know if people remember the scenes of the dust coming down a road and people running away from it. Well, that was the road the hotel was on that I stayed at. It got really shaken by the blast, so much so they didn't know if the building was going to be condemned along with some of the others. It's built of sheer black glass. It felt very strange to be there. It really made an impression on me ... to play my part in understanding the devastation and effect of how 9/11 had completely floored New York and the USA. It was very humbling.

And the amount of Limos that came and went, at all times, day and night. They were obviously pulling up to pay their respects to lost loved ones. It's the only place I've been to in New York where silence reigned, like a dark cloud hovering ... Still ... unearthly ... unreal ... yet thick with atmosphere, almost suffocating. What a place, as if suspended in time. It sent shivers down my spine. A profound experience.

It is a rare person indeed who walks away from that place unaffected. Yet there was hope; a long, long line of drawings on the entire side of the perimeter fence lovingly created by the children and the people. Such respect and honour for those that lost their lives on that tragic day of 9/11. Yet life goes on ...

I got my first few bookings through advertising on *Eros*. It was so very exciting. And my very first booking –the very first one! – was someone who wanted to be '*trampled*'! Not wanting to turn anyone away, I accepted the booking to do some trampling. I had never ever done it before!

So! steve and I started practicing. We practiced for hours and hours. Poor him ! I just kept trampling all over him. He loved it! When trampling someone, there are certain places of the body that you can't trample and there are some places that are better than others, like the bottom, or the top of the back. I was very careful, but I'm not the most balanced person ... nor the lightest! He had to lie down next to the wardrobe so I could hang on to the wardrobe door. We had such fun and games, laughing, doing this trampling, getting ready, and then at the last minute the guy cancelled! I'd done all this trampling practice for absolutely nothing ... but we had fun doing it.

I also had a booking from somebody who wanted to be caned. At that time there weren't many Mistresses who did caning. Rather than sending him up to the room, I sent steve down to Reception to meet him. He showed him to the room then lurked, very discreetly, out of the way and out of the room. The gentleman who'd turned up must've come from the docks. He wore this green wax jacket and a little pork pie type hat. He was quite a brash New Yorker and came out with, "Right, okay, I'll let you know. I'd like to try some caning," in his rough American accent.

I told him to bend over the bed. Obviously he had to take his coat off, which he took off with theatrical aplomb and threw it on the bed. Then he took off his hat and nonchalantly tossed that on the bed. *There should've been music to this,* I thought irritatedly, poised with my cane and tapping my foot, *he's taking too long!* Next, he took his phone out of his pocket and threw it on top of his hat. Finally, in one fell swoop, he dropped his trousers and bent over the bed. *Now!* I thought, then proceeded to cane him.

Well! Two things happened during the caning session. First of all, earlier I had reported something wrong with the room to Reception and two maintenance men, unbeknownst to me, had turned up unexpectedly to mend whatever it was, a light or something like that, in the room.

Steve, who had hidden very discreetly out of the way, saw them arrive but obviously didn't want to interfere. He didn't want to be seen at all! They knocked on the door, right in the middle of my caning six strokes! I paused but didn't answer. I carried on caning, and they knocked again! steve, who was watching them, told me later that apparently they'd heard the caning, looked at each other, then said, "Let's come back later," and hurried away, which I found highly amusing thinking about it afterwards!

Incredibly, there was yet more interruption! And it wasn't even a long session! The guy's phone rang – he hadn't put it on silent!

"Can you hang on a minute," he said, reaching for his phone. Then he answered it! So there he was, bare bottomed, bent over the bed having a brief business meeting during a very brief caning! Then he turned to me and said, "I've got to go now. I'll speak to you later." And he left! *He didn't spend long putting his clothes back on,* I thought wryly. It *was* really funny though. That was my first proper session in New York. So eventful! Definitely one I'll never forget!

Making the most of New York, I visited a fetish club nearby. It wasn't that far away from where I was. It was called *'Paddles'*. You went down the stairs into a basement and ... what an amazing place! I loved going to *Paddles.* Once inside the nightclub, there was a door in the basement that led through to another dungeon area available for hire.

That was called *'Pandora's Box'*. It was a well-run and very popular establishment owned and run by *Mistress Raven*, a lovely lady. She was spot on with everything. Her venue did well, and deservedly so. I went to *Paddles* every time I could, whenever I was in New York.

One Thursday a month, *Paddles* had an education slot, and I used to try and coincide my visits with that particular Thursday. I'd fly over on the Thursday and, despite feeling really tired, it was well worth it. It was a highly educational event, professionally hosted by a well organised group of people called *'TES'*, which stands for *'The Eulenspiegel Society'*. They still run it to this day.

One thing I like about the USA and its people is that they like to learn, and they like to do things properly. And I used to love going to *Paddles.*

During my time there, I'd been having friendly chats with another Mistress called *Mistress Elizabeth Roze,* who lived on Long Island. She invited us to visit her at her home. We caught the train from the very famous Penn Street Station to Amityville. Whenever you see movies on location, you always see trains to Amityville. I had a sense of déjà vu while waiting at the station. It all felt so familiar to me.

I boarded the train with my sub. What very strange trains they have, nothing like the ones in the UK. I seem to remember it had five seats together on one side of the train, then the gangway, flanked by two, three or four seats together on the other. They were pure commuter trains going in and out of New York.

We informed *Mistress Elizabeth Roze* what time we were catching the train so she could meet us at the station with an expected time of arrival. She had told us where to get off before it reached Amityville, so when we got there, I found it really strange. The train was standing on a twenty- or thirty-foot-high concrete platform. All you had was this narrow platform, then down a set of steps to get off the train.

We were the only people that got off the train. There was nobody there. We couldn't see anybody. Then a couple of minutes later, a great big Mercedes pulled up. A guy got out and approached us.

"Are you Mistress Susan?"

"Yes, I am."

"Come with me. Mistress has sent me to come pick you up."

How bizarre! So, there we were, in a complete stranger's car in New York, completely on trust. He did take us to see the most dignified and proper lady, who had what appeared to be a single-story property with a discreet basement transformed into a dungeon. It was lovely to talk to her. She's an absolutely lovely lady.

Mistresses, you know ... there are some real characters. I mean real characters! *Mistress Elizabeth Roze*, she even gave me a few of her toys. Obviously taking things back to the UK was difficult for me due to lack of space and luggage weight, but the USA toys she gave me I still have to this day. What a day we had! The same driver took us back to the station and we caught the train back on a high!

We had a great time in New York. I had quite a few sessions, which covered all my core costs such as flight, travel, hotel and so forth. It whetted my appetite to do even more. I was loving it. I was hooked.

Ah yes, while we were there, we also visited a world-famous dungeon that was available to hire called 'The Nutcracker Suite'. You could see the Empire State Building from there and the dungeon comprised of lots and lots of different rooms. We had ourselves a lovely session. Just wonderful.

It was all about getting to know the area. With New York, it's good because there are plenty of landmarks that became useful compass points, so we couldn't get lost. This one being so close to the Empire State Building was perfect for that.

On walkabout we discovered a BDSM shop on the Upper East Side. We did a lot of walking while travelling around, familiarising ourselves with New York. It was really good. Very useful. And the hotel we stayed in was amazing.

We bought the most amazing suitcase from Century 21, a famous shop next door to my hotel, within a very tall building in New York. The suitcase looked like a huge rucksack on wheels. You could get so much stuff in it! It was really long and took all my canes; it was great! Pulling it along on wheels when it was weighed down with all my canes was a godsend. It was just like pulling a trolley. Marvellous! They sold all kinds of stuff in that shop. It was like something out of wonderland, but for adults. Amazing.

The monetary exchange rate at that time was two dollars to the pound. It was really good value to the pound – things were so much cheaper over in America. What a wonderful time we had over there! It gave me the taste for America, and the people were so nice, they really were.

That was my first visit over the pond, and I thoroughly enjoyed it. I intended to return for more, and I did. I wasn't disappointed.

Chapter Seventeen

Los Angeles: First DomCon Trip

I'd become quite friendly with *Madam A*, whom I'd met through the Judicial Punishment Training dungeon, and as we chatted away she had told me about something called the *'DomCon'* in Los Angeles. She said she was thinking of going, and did I fancy going with her?

It sounded really interesting, so I did my own research, got the website details up and looked into it. It looked fantastic! The Americans do like their conventions. They have all sorts of conventions for all sorts of things; you name it, they do it.

It was held over four days, maybe five nights, and was jam-packed with demonstrations, workshops, discussion groups, even a market selling BDSM equipment. But what intrigued me the most is that Day One was devoted to Industry-Only Pro-Dommes. It sounded amazing! *I'm going!* I thought, *It sounds great!* And it was! I wasn't disappointed.

It's quite a long way to LA on the plane, so I flew to New York and stayed over for a few days with one of my subs, Mikey, who I mention in another chapter. We spent two or three days together, having a good time in New York. He lived out in the suburbs of Westchester County in a nice ground floor flat in a peaceful area. It was lovely.

I caught the plane from New York to LA. I think it was about a four-hour internal flight. America is so big, people fly everywhere. LAX Airport was just opposite the hotel where the *DomCon* was being held. Perfect!

The lady who created and still runs *DomCon* is called *Mistress Cyan*. *Mistress Cyan* is transgender and a lovely lady. She is quite a figure; very imposing. She is very tall and very well organised. I must say she has a really good organisational team that arranges this event every year, and I think by now it's probably on about its twelfth year! A real success.

The Industry-Only talks provided a fantastic platform to talk among other Pro-Dommes. Virtually all of them were from America. The Americans are different to the Brits. The Mistresses are all about putting on the glitz, 'showing off, for want of a better word. They were all about showing their best face and prancing around to varying degrees. That doesn't mean they didn't know their business; oh yes, they certainly did know about making money, and by doing things professionally as well.

I'm different. I didn't exactly fit in because I wasn't prepared to wear corsets all the time. A flashy image wasn't so important to me; it was what I did that was important. I have never been one to show off, not from my childhood 'til now. For me, it's about what's on the inside, not the outside.

I got on well with the other Pro-Dommes, though. I made friends with *Mistress Jade* from Hawaii; *Mistress Precious*; and a Mistress from Washington who had previously lived close to the White House but had relocated to the West Coast. I think she was called *Mistress Ellen*. All sorts of different people. There was one called *Mistress Phoenix* as well, if I remember rightly.

The Mistresses that were all about their image didn't bother with me. I wasn't about to further their careers being seen around me, so they left me alone. Just the way I like it, under the radar …

There were lots and lots of people there and I learned a great deal. There was a lot to absorb. A lot to take in. During a conversation with a group of Mistresses, I had mentioned that a while ago, I'd heard from somebody who said he wanted to be 'ironed', way back in the early days of my entering into this lifestyle. I thought he was just kidding me! *Ironed! Ironed!* I thought, *Is he crazy? He's got to be making this up!*

Anyway, one of the Mistresses from New York piped up and told me that he was actually a genuine person! A bona fide client! I thought that was quite amazing. How incredible someone wanted to go to such lengths. So extreme! I had no idea people actually wanted to be branded, ironed, for real. *That's way off the scale,* I thought to myself with a shrug, *each to his own I guess.* But wow! It just goes to show, you just never can tell!

That was a big lesson for me. People want all sorts of weird and wonderful experiences, and just because we don't understand or agree with them, well, we shouldn't dismiss them. We're not right and they're wrong. Or vice versa. We're all different, and that's what makes this lifestyle and life in general so diverse. Rich and uniquely different. Without all these differences, wouldn't life be boring?!

The workshops themselves were incredible. There were three different areas where they held these workshops. They were held back-to-back. You name it, they had workshops on it. They covered various aspects of Health and Safety; Relationships; Dynamics; and Play, in a 'How To ...' approach. They were all excellent and really informative.

They included Polyamory; Role-play; even 'Extreme Play'! They also held play parties in the evenings; Mistress Tea Parties; Mistress-Only events; Leather events ... it was packed! And it was filled back-to-back with stuff to do. I actually don't think I had to buy a ticket for some reason, though I can't remember why.

One of the events I went to in the evening was at *Mistress Cyan's* dungeon studio, called *'Sanctuary'*.

One evening I saw *Mistress Cyan* standing on the stage, Florentine Flogging somebody; a two-handed, rhythmic flogging using matching floggers, inspired by a double sword formal salute from Kung-Fu. I was totally mesmerised! The flogging was completely in unison. It was absolutely spell-binding. In those days Florentine Flogging was rarely seen; nowadays it's commonplace. It takes a long time to perfect, but it's awesome, mindful even.

I spoke to *Mistress Cyan* afterwards and she invited me back to the next *DomCon* to host a caning workshop and also to be Guest of Honour at the *DomCon* LA! What an honour! I thought it was tremendous!

I had a few clients while in LA, so that made up my spending money. I managed to buy lots of things at the *DomCon Fair* out of my earnings, which was great. It was a great way to build up my equipment. All the gear I bought was, of course, top quality.

I was given lots of tips about how the system operates when I was there, including putting me onto this service that a lot of the Pro-Dommes were members of, called 'Niteflirt'; a telephone domination/sex chat service. It was a sex chatline, really, but included a BDSM section. People could phone up for a specific form of BDSM that was catered to suit specific requirements, and even went as far as providing corporal punishment (CP) chat and the like.

I took their advice and enrolled into *Niteflirt.* I'm so glad I did, because I actually made enough money to pay for my next trip to LA through it. Incredible! I used to get calls from specific people who liked my English accent. They would phone me up and I would dominate them online. They would mark me as a favourite and then when I logged on to accept calls, they would call me.

I had a few regulars; some in the US who were more into fantasy and imagination stories, and some in the UK who leaned toward the 'strict schoolmistress' types of scenarios. One guy who travelled all over the US used to call me for about half an hour at a time from wherever he was, even when I was back in the UK! He got off on me talking and smoking while blowing out the smoke so he could hear it. Of course, I had to have the kitchen window open, but I didn't tell him that!

It was good fun, actually. I didn't have to log in at any particular time and I had licence to just log in whenever I had a few minutes spare.

I also had quite a few subs in America I'd been in contact with online. One of them was a Brit who lived in a place close to LA. He came to see me when I was there, for a caning. He was ex-Navy and knew Plymouth, where I used to live. He was involved in the BDSM community but had relocated to America when he retired. I'm still in contact with him to this day.

He makes personalised canes and whips and gave me a few of his canes to take home as well as a lovely American snake whip.

Such a wonderful gesture. Americans are very generous people and very friendly. He had integrated so well there you would think he was a natural born American! But, of course, he wasn't.

During my stay, I took a round trip on one of LA's small tour buses, kind of similar to our open-top buses, and got to see all the places of interest, like Hollywood Boulevard and Rodeo Drive with all its magnificent shops. We were shown where all the rich actors and famous people live; the famous handprints on the Hollywood Walk of Fame. All places of interest. It also took us to Santa Monica Boulevard. You could get on and off this tour bus at any time, so I got off the bus and walked up Santa Monica Boulevard. What a place! For me it was amazing!

I don't know why I felt it was so amazing; perhaps because it's a part of America, and maybe partly because these places seem so familiar, with hearing about them in songs or seeing them in films. But it was a lovely, open, happy place to walk along. I thoroughly enjoyed it.

On my second trip to *DomCon*, I walked down Santa Monica Boulevard again, and this time I walked to the end of the boulevard, where I saw a Rastafarian fisherman, fishing. *Fishing! At the end of a boulevard! Wow!* It looked more like a pier in the harbour to me. He had really long dreadlocks and a bucket by his side.

I walked up to him. "What fish have you caught?" I asked.

"A mackerel," he answered back with a grin.

Well, I thought, *you come all this way from Great Britain to the other side of America and he catches a mackerel! Mackerels must be everywhere. How bizarre!*

DomCon in LA was an amazing place, but LAX Airport certainly wasn't! The people on security were rude. They re-routed you all over the place and you had a really long way to walk. The security system wasn't very good when I was there, either. Staff would send your bags outside onto an island where anyone could walk in and out with easy access. It was very strange.

All the while, of course, there were Celebs coming and going. Although you or I may not recognise them, you could tell they were Celebs because they either had security with them, or they had a limo pulled up by the islands with the doors open, just outside from where you reclaimed your luggage; either that or the paparazzi were waiting for them ... how tiresome!

The Celebs were always surrounded by paparazzi. They used to come running out to avoid them. It was quite funny actually; one of the Celebs came running out to avoid the cameras, running quite fast, but her Limo wasn't there so she had to run back in again! That made me chuckle. It just seemed quite bizarre. I bet the driver got quite an earful! I could have helped and given him a caning ... If only they knew! Quite unrelated to my life, but a funny experience anyway!

Needless to say, I thoroughly enjoyed *DomCon* in LA. Flying back, I took the direct flight to Heathrow. It's a long-haul flight; I think it took ten or eleven hours. The flights from LA were always full, so I didn't get lots of leg room. I had been okay going over because I'd stopped off at New York on the way.

It may have been a long-haul flight going home, but it was worth it. I made a lot of friends in LA. It was all very interesting.

Chapter Eighteen

New York: Sex Slave

I used to love going to New York. I aimed for five trips per year. I was getting quite used to travelling to New York and soon found more economical ways of getting there and where to stay. I used to try and stay somewhere different every time.

I found out it was cheaper to fly into Newark Airport – it's still a New York Airport, but it's on the other side of the Hudson River. It's in New Jersey, and so I began to stay in New Jersey, an area very close to Central New York. You could either drive through one of the tunnels in a car or jump on a train and go across the Hudson to Penn St Station, which was quite central.

When I first started going over and staying in New Jersey, I used to catch one of the trains that went across the river and came up through *Ground Zero.* That was a very strange feeling. A feeling of sadness and emptiness. It felt surreal being so close to that landmark of devastation.

It was much quicker to get around from New Jersey than in downtown New York where, in certain places, the traffic was quite heavy. I got more and more used to New York and the surrounding areas. I just loved staying in the different places with their diverse and interesting culture, seeing how and where people lived and worked.

I think part of what I enjoyed was that you always feel like you've been to New York before. Everything is so familiar! I think it's because so many films and US television series are filmed there. I can recognise places so easily!

I loved going to Central Park, with its view of the *Apple Shop* sitting right on the outskirts of it; a prominent backdrop with its sheer glass … the entire building! Amazing. Then there was *Tiffany's* … I even saw *Donald Trump* close to *Trump Tower*! Obviously, it was a long time ago. I doubt he walks anywhere now except his golf course! The *Russian Tearooms, Staten Island Ferry,* watching talented musicians and dancers on the subway … I loved every bit of it!

Every time I went over the *Pond*, I incorporated social time as well as booking my sessions. I met a slave over there called Stewart. I got on very well with him; I thought he was a lovely man. He was in construction, and, like a lot of other people in New York, he had a second job to earn more money. Stewart's second job was driving limos. One of his regular customers was a *huge* rock star. He was hired to drive him to the airport and back on all his trips.

A lovely man. He loved his motorbikes; he owned several. He used to drive me all over New York and New Jersey – in his pick-up, not on his bike! He took me to shopping malls; to diners, to eat typical American food. He also used to take me to my favourite restaurant in New York, '*Le Pain Quotidien*'. He took me there one Sunday. We drove over from New Jersey to New York, to the restaurant, which was very near Central Park, just on the corner of 7th Avenue. You could walk there from Central Park.

On this particular Sunday, he drove around and around looking for somewhere to park his car in New York. It was a nightmare! An absolute nightmare! I can't remember if the car parks were closed, or if they were just ridiculously expensive. He was convinced he would find a parking space. Eventually we found one and enjoyed a lovely lunch in my favourite restaurant.

Afterwards we went for a stroll to the *Apple Shop* at the top of Central Park. It was such a lovely day … until we returned to the car and found he'd got a parking ticket! I think it was something ridiculous – like a $110 fine! It was crazy. I felt awful, but he said it was worth it.

By far, Stewart's best asset was: he had the hardest cock I had ever, ever known. It was rock hard! Basically, I'd just tie him to the bed and sit on his cock riding him in triumph.

"This isn't about you, this is about me, and I am enjoying it!" I'd say wildly, and with that, his cock would get even harder! He is the one and only sub that I've ever had as a sex slave. It had always been my 'rule of thumb' to refrain from sex with any BDSM client of mine, but this was for my pleasure alone. I really liked him. He was really pleasurable and so much fun! I guess that was obvious.

He used to pick me up from the airport in New Jersey; sometimes it was quick to get through Immigration, sometimes it wasn't. It was generally quick though. He had always said to me, "If you ever get stopped, you must tell them that you're coming to meet me, but don't tell them what we do. Please? They just won't be able to get their heads around that." He'd given me his address, just in case Immigration asked, because he knew what they were like.

This one time, I got stopped at Immigration. The guy was asking me all sorts of very well calculated questions you just couldn't lie to. Of course, they were merely doing their job ...

"Why have you come here on your own?"

"I've come to meet a man-friend."

"Well how did you meet him?"

"I met him online," I answered truthfully.

"You should be careful doing that. Where does he live?"

"Is that an alright area?" I asked after showing him the address.

"Hmm. Yeah, it's okay," in his curt American accent. "It's okay." Then he ushered me through. That incident left me feeling a bit hot under the collar. The interrogation was really uncomfortable; it took me a while to come down from that.

There are some classic photographs of New York at night that are fantastic. One of them is taken from the bottom of New York, looking up into Manhattan. That skyline is the most popular photograph. But I prefer the skyline photograph taken from the New Jersey side. At one particular point I told Stewart, "I'd love a photograph of that skyline. It's so amazing," as I looked on in awe.

After we'd been out to dinner one night, it was pitch black. We were going back to the hotel, driving on quite a precarious road in his 4x4 open truck, when suddenly he pulled the truck over onto the hard shoulder, jumped into the back of it, and took a photograph of the skyline for me. I thought he was very brave. Unfortunately, the photograph didn't turn out very well. It would have been a lovely shot; I would've liked to have got a clear photograph of that.

Stewart was my sex slave. I really liked him. He wanted to retire to Western Virginia, to buy a shack in the middle of a field and just go live there. He was a nice guy. I liked him a lot. I would have gone with him if he had asked, but he didn't …

There was another submissive I'd been messaging right from the beginning called Mikey, who used to come over and see me in New Jersey. He also used to pick me up from the airport or take me back, whenever Stewart wasn't available. He used to tell me his tales and I swear, if I hadn't heard it from his mouth, I'd never have believed it at that stage of my journey into BDSM.

He was a lovely lad. He used to run a website; that's how he earned his living. I didn't know how he did it. He didn't appear to be super clever, but I think he was a bit of a gambler. It was him I stayed with on my way to my first DomCon, as I mentioned in a previous chapter. He made me feel very welcome. I had a lovely time.

I knew him for quite a few years. He was a good lad. He was looking for something, but didn't know exactly what. It helped him a great deal to talk to me, to investigate his feelings a little bit more. That was Mikey.

Chapter Nineteen

Los Angeles: DomCon:
Second Trip and Vegas

On my second visit to *DomCon* in LA, I had been invited to be 'Guest of Honour' and to hold a caning workshop. It really was a great honour. I decided to go with my other *Twisted Sister, Mistress Torment*. I thought we might be able to get a few sessions to help pay for it, although for me, it was already paid for through my clients from *Niteflirt*.

We went along to the *DomCon* and it didn't disappoint. It was the same magic, second time around.

The Americans are different to us. I find that so interesting. Different people's cultures fascinate me. I just love to immerse myself in other people's culture. You can always learn something from the way people do things; provided you have an open and enquiring mind, of course.

One of the things I found quite fascinating was that the *DomCon* was being held quite openly in the hotel, but within an absolutely enormous basement. There were two conventions being held at the same time in the basement that day. Neither of the conventions opened until eleven o'clock in the morning, so there was a queue of people patiently waiting, side by side, for the doors to open and enter their convention; one for the *DomCon*, and the other? A religious convention! How bizarre.

Incredibly, there was one queue of people dressed in outrageous finery of Gothic outfits, corsets, leather, tattoos, piercings ... it was amazing; and then the other queue full of religious people, pretty much all dressed conservatively. A stark contrast indeed to the clothes that the *DomCon* people were wearing as they stood all lined up next to each other. It still makes me chuckle.

And you know what the thing about America is? You're allowed to have different opinions. You're allowed to have freedom of thought and speech. No-one can be denied that. It's one of the principles in their *Freedom of Speech* law of civil liberty. Nobody criticised, either person nor either group, for anything. I really valued that. This was a common cultural difference throughout the USA in every area.

As advertised in the *DomCon* Presentation Official Program of 2009, I held my caning session workshop at the allotted time of 5.30–6.30 that Friday evening. We took Andrew with us as my submissive, and my friend who lived in Palm Springs. He also came along so I could demonstrate on his bottom at my workshop. The caning class was full, and both bottoms came in very useful!

The Americans at that time weren't really *au fait* with caning, so they were all very keen and interested to have an expert 'in the field', direct from the UK. You can cane most places on the body, but one place you should *always* avoid is the kidneys. You should avoid the kidneys *at all costs*. It's an important safety aspect in caning. I remember asking them such a question on caning:

"There's only one place on the human body that you're not supposed to cane because it's dangerous. Can anybody tell what that place is?"

Somebody put their hand up and said, "Their face?"

I didn't expect that! It was quite funny. That was one of the contrasts between USA and the UK – no one in UK would say that, or even think of it. But the Americans did! I guess they tend to be more outspoken and outrageous than us. Good for them!

I made friends with a few Mistresses who wanted to learn all about English caning, and was asked if I would come back over and do some sessions with them and some of their clients. They liked the *English Rose* type of thing. That was a great acknowledgement and excellent feedback; they obviously appreciated my caning expertise. I had a lovely time there.

I remember, at the end of *DomCon,* they held a group photoshoot with all the Mistresses who had attended, to appear in the next year's program. Well, *Mistress Torment* and I didn't realise what it was all about, so we didn't particularly dress up. We just wore our 'working office' gear that we generally wear to a CP session. When we went downstairs for the shoot, however, we discovered every Mistress was done up – absolutely done-up to the nines! They were really out there to outshine everybody else.

It just looked like *Mistress Torment* and I had walked right in off the street and entered the wrong room by mistake! We look so out of place! It was so funny! I don't think they put that particular photograph into the next year's program, but it was quite funny! We looked like interlopers! It still makes me chuckle to think about it!

After *DomCon* was over, we had booked up to stay in Las Vegas for a three- or four-night visit while we were in the vicinity. We had arranged some appointments in Vegas, which helped cover the cost and pay our way. Strangely enough, one of our appointments was a guy fromWales, who used to drive heavy haulage for the Defence Industry all across America. Their articulated lorries are absolutely huge! He had his session, and *Mistress Torment* and I thought how bizarre it was that we had to go all the way to Vegas to see somebody who came from a few hundred miles up the road from us!

I always plan in advance, so I had contacted a submissive guy from Vegas whom I'd been writing to online, to arrange to meet up while we were there. Well, he showed us all over Las Vegas throughout our entire trip! How fantastic was that?! He took us to the shops; he took us out to the theatre; he took us out for meals; to shows at the casinos, and even took us to the Gaming Casinos outside the main Vegas Strip. I *loved* going to the casinos.

We saw much more of Vegas than the usual holidaymaker. He even showed us where all the gangs were – there's lots of gangs in Vegas. It's not quite as it is purported to be on the TV. Once you get outside of the *Strip*, it's a totally different world.

He took us to a Lighting Show in a canopied area in Fremont St, in downtown Las Vegas. It was an evening spectacle; an open-air planetarium of the night sky and the stars, thunder, storms, things like that. It's quite famous and just down the road from that place where everybody gets married in Vegas.

We managed to go to a few munches as well. Munches are always a great way of meeting like-minded people in the BDSM scene for drinks and a chat. It's almost always held in a vanilla setting. Again, I found the Americans so different. They're more light-hearted, yet serious. There was an element of fun, and yet they took it all very, very seriously. It was good seeing the diversity of the people. I enjoyed that aspect.

In this lifestyle you can meet people that you would never meet in your normal everyday life. You could be anywhere in the world and still have that common ground to talk about things, and because respecting differences without judging is at the core of the BDSM lifestyle, people welcomed you and generally trusted you. Quite refreshing, I must say.

We stayed in my usual hotel chain, but not one on the *Strip*. It was half the price! It had a lovely swimming pool and was much quieter, and as we had a local submissive at our beck and call, it didn't really matter about activities, because he chauffeured us around absolutely everywhere.

It was a great part of the trip, getting to know the area. The one thing we didn't do, but I wish we had, was book a helicopter ride to the Grand Canyon; but there's always another time for that.

I had a little chuckle to myself at the airport on my return home. I had my canes in my canvas snooker cue bag, perfect for carrying them around undetected. It was as long as any fishing rod. I'd had them couriered over for *DomCon* but hadn't arranged to courier them back. So, at the airport, when the check-in clerk said, "Thank you, ma'am." as she handed me back my passport, I mused to myself, *interesting turn of address,* and was caught unprepared when she asked, "And what do you have in your bag?"

"Canes," I replied automatically. *Damn!* I thought, *What will they do now? Confiscate them?* I felt the panic rising up inside me, but she didn't bat an eyelid!

"Enjoy your flight," was all she said with a smile before ushering me through.

Another example of the freedom you have in the US. No judgement whatsoever. Very refreshing. What a beautiful Country.

Chapter Twenty

New York. Returning Home

I can't say it enough; I just loved going to New York. Like I said, I tried to go five times per year. I had to pre-book my tickets up to a year in advance to get seats at a reasonable cost to keep my travel budget down. That wasn't a problem for me, as I had to schedule all my travels ... Glasgow, London, Leeds, Birmingham ... all over, so it was never a problem.

As I've said, I got really good at travelling across to New York. I used to always fly in to Newark Airport, New Jersey. It was much easier to get to and I used to stay in hotels in New Jersey, always my favourite brand of course! I tried to stay in different ones every time.

I remember one flight, the weather was absolutely dreadful all over the UK. It was a countrywide problem. I was catching the last flight out from Heathrow that evening, which meant I'd arrive in New Jersey very late. It was very windy. Flights were getting cancelled or delayed left, right and centre. Total chaos!

My flight departure was delayed slightly, so by the time we got to Heathrow, it took ages to land. That was normal procedure whenever there was a backlog. Needless to say, I missed my connecting flight to New York, as did lots of other people. We were directed somewhere to change our tickets and there was a massive queue; not surprising when there were so many cancellations and missed connections.

There were a lot of Americans in the queue, and Americans just do not like queuing! I think they call it standing in a line. I didn't like queuing either, if the truth is to be known, but there wasn't anything any of us could do, so I resigned myself to just accept the inevitable and go with it. They were doing their best. The ground crew were totally overwhelmed.

An American lady in the queue, two people in front of me, was really angry. She made it known that she was angry; everyone heard her. She gave the booking assistant hell! She was informed she had to stay overnight in London to enable her to catch her plane the next morning, and the airline were happy to put her up in a hotel, free of charge. They booked her in a hotel thirty or forty miles away from London.

"Well how am I going to get there?!" she demanded.

"Get a taxi. You can reclaim the taxi money. Just make sure you get a receipt." They weren't particularly helpful to her, but they did what they had to do.

My turn now, I thought as I approached the Reception desk, *God, where the hell am I gonna end up? A hotel in the back of beyond?* I really felt for the staff because they were getting a lot of gyp from the Americans, they really were.

"It's awful, isn't it? I know you're doing your best," I said sympathetically as they rescheduled my flight to a morning flight.

"Do you want to stay in a hotel?"

"Yes please. I usually stay in Hiltons, if it's at all possible?"

"Sure," *she* said amicably, then promptly booked me into the Hilton at Heathrow Airport Terminal Five. I didn't even have to get a taxi! It was within walking distance and so close to the take-off terminal. *You know what,* I thought, *sometimes it's nice to be nice. It's always nice to be nice, but sometimes it's important to be nice.*

For every hotel I booked when I stayed in New Jersey, I afforded myself a great deal of time to explore the local areas, which I really enjoyed. One was at Path Station, near Hoboken. The hotel was just across the road from the station. I could catch a train that went over the Hudson, which then took a right turn, and, at that time, continued to the World Trade Centre, right on the perimeter of where it was being demolished. It gave me a completely new vantage point of the whole demolition process as it unfolded. It's such an eerie place to be in, but that route took me directly into Central New York quickly and easily. A cinch, really.

I stayed all over New Jersey. Another place I liked staying was located near the Trotting Racecourse Track. There were a few stadiums in that area; I think one was a Baseball Stadium. Anyway, the trotting horses were there, and I used to be able to see them from my window, exercising in the mornings. I really enjoyed that. It was great! Being a proficient horse rider myself, I really appreciated the spectacle of the display before me. I stayed there quite a few times because of that.

To sum it all up, I used to get to stay in all the different hotels and got to know my way around New York. I had my favourite restaurant which I used to go to on 7th Avenue, then continue from there straight into *Paddles* near 8th Avenue to coincide with my visits with the *Paddles* lectures organised by *TES*.

I remember attending their *Trampling Workshop* directly from the airport! My sex slave rushed me there just in time. The lady holding the lecture was mesmerising! Amazing! She was so informative, telling you where you could stand, where you couldn't stand, why you couldn't stand there. You know you can do some serious damage to somebody. She was so good, so knowledgeable, and so light-footed! It was almost like she was floating … like a dancer. It was amazing to watch.

I loved learning in New York. They had a slightly different twist on things, and they're very open to education. I enjoyed that aspect of it.

I had lots of clients that came to me too; all sorts of different people. I was the perfect Mistress for some 'body'. I was an unknown face in the USA. I didn't know any of my clients, and nobody really knew me either; so if somebody wanted complete anonymity, that was great for me and ideal for them.

One guy, I remember, had a fetish for having his body hair shaved off. He used to have his own 'buzzer', as he called it, and I shaved off his body hair with it. I had another guy who came down from Washington who just wanted to worship my feet. He would knock on the door, I'd open it, then he'd throw himself on the floor, crawl across the floor and spend thirty minutes kissing my feet. Then he left; simple as that.

I had one guy who used to book two-hour sessions with me. I quite liked him actually. He was a youngish man – in his thirties – who liked to talk; and he talked and he talked and he talked and he talked ... Then we used to follow it up with a session where he liked to bend over the suitcase packing station, which is often in front of a mirror, and have me spank or cane his arse. He used to have me peg him as well.

One day, he told me he wanted to phone his wife and have me grab hold of his genitals and squeeze them while he talked to her on the phone! To this day I still don't know what he got from that, but he obviously got something from it. He was quite a deep person. We used to spend a lot of time talking. Whatever he got from it must've been really important to him. I still don't understand why, but that's for him to know. I know for sure he enjoyed the thrill of it all.

My clients were a diverse mix. All sorts of people, all sorts of ages, in all sorts of jobs, and I found it fascinating. My sex slave used to take me out to dinner, and it was so interesting to talk about what the Americans really think; their views on different people, politics, the healthcare, taxes, unions, stuff like that. I thoroughly enjoyed learning about their difference in culture and understanding their viewpoints and opinions on my visits.

On all my flights to and from New York, I used to ask for a seat at the back of the plane. Because they were very big planes, by the time I got to the back of the plane, if the flight to New York wasn't full, I was more likely to get a whole row of seats to myself. Flying to New York, there were so many flights a day that the flights never seemed to be full. As a result, I was often able to move the arm rests on three seats, lie down and go to sleep for a few hours. That was great! It really suited me, because of the time difference.

The return flight was just as advantageous. The bonus of being at the back of the plane was the fact I got off last. Business Class passengers were always given complimentary toiletry bags. Often when walking through Business Class, there were all these discarded and unopened 'goody bags' left behind from frequent travellers.

Well, I used to pick one up now and again. That used to make my trip! Isn't it funny how it's the little things you get such a buzz from? It made me feel like I'd travelled Business Class when I'd bagged three seats to myself and then got a 'goody bag' at the end of it. It was great! That was good fun. Such a treat! Everyone likes a freebie!

Despite the fun, it was a long old trip because the connecting flight couldn't be booked any earlier than ninety minutes later because of the transfer times at Heathrow Airport. There weren't as many connecting flights; that was the only downside. Sometimes I had to wait two to three hours for the final leg of my journey. I didn't really mind though; it gave me time to think, to process my trip. I was happy. It was great fun people watching. I loved it!

I loved America and everything to do with it; it was exciting, different, educational, and invigorating. I always think of the song, 'New York, New York' – "If I can make it there, I'll make it anywhere ..." Well, I made it in New York. I even bought a New York cellphone with a New York *917* number! When I arrived in the US, I loved switching it on and listening to all my messages. More bookings, yay!

Unfortunately, my messages weren't all good. The way the cellphone system works in the US is that after a certain amount of time, the numbers get put back into the system and re-allocated; it was my luck to get someone who hadn't paid his debts! The phone calls! Some of them were really not very nice ... but that's all history now!

Looking back, I *did* feel I made it in New York. I didn't make loads of money in New York, but it funded my travels; I met some fabulous people; I was very comfortable and familiar with it all; I knew my way around New York City; and I learned about the culture. Yes, I made it in New York. And I'm very proud of that. Very proud.

Chapter Twenty-One

Mistress Breaks

When I first started setting up my purpose-built dungeon up north, we used to run an event once a month on a Friday evening called *Single Subs Night*. A handful of Mistresses would turn up and practice on a variety of different subs who'd attended. Practice, practice, practice was the theme of the session. The Mistresses had a great time honing their skills, and the subs enjoyed their punishment. It was a good event all round, most enjoyable.

The venue owner held a Swingers Club that ran upstairs at the same time as our event in the dungeon on a Friday and used to allow us to share the bar area and basement. He also had a big screen and would play DVDs down in the basement. Well, we claimed that and used to commandeer it for our particular brand of fetish DVDs.

Swingers being swingers and the friendly souls that they are, they used to be nosey and come into the basement room to chat with us; well, the guys did! Brash and full of inquisitiveness, they used to insist on staying and watching our DVDs. Well, the looks on their faces when they saw people being caned or teased … or worse! The smiles were frozen to their faces and the laughter was most definitely forced! Not wanting to lose face of course, it was amazing how some of them used to quietly slip out of the room to escape the possibility of us catching them and asking them to join in! So funny!

Following that, I started to organise a *'Mistress 'Weekend' Break'*. Not an actual weekend as such, because the hotel was used Friday and Saturday nights, but the rest of the week was free, so I used to hold the *Mistress Break* from Sunday evening to Wednesday morning for three nights, as if it were a weekend.

Six to eight Mistresses used to come along with their subs, as well as volunteer maids and volunteer slaves. Typically, Sunday evening would begin with a meeting so all the Mistresses could get to know each other over a few drinks. Generally a good chatty evening, really. The event, though, was a fully catered, lavish affair.

On arrival, Mistresses each received a personalised *'Welcome Itinerary Menu'* from which to select throughout the duration of their stay, explaining dining arrangements and schedules; entertainment; and room service information, as well as the facilities available and the slaves at their disposal.

An allotted sub would come and take the Mistresses' breakfast orders from the breakfast menu I provided the night before, then, every morning, they would get up very early to prepare whatever it was the Mistresses decided they'd want for breakfast.

The breakfasts were generally taken in the Mistresses' rooms, although they could eat downstairs if they preferred. Afterwards we would have 'roll-call', where all the slaves and submissives would line up in the dungeon for inspection to check whether they were 'fit for service'. Rituals are important, especially to 'Old School' Mistresses like myself. I had all sorts; a ritual to start a session, a ritual to finish, rituals when caning, counting the strokes, rituals to greet … the list can be endless. It's an integral part of the loss of control that appeals to many.

If they weren't suitably attired, or not attired at all, they would be punished with the implement decided by whoever was doing the roll-call. We used to take it in turns, a couple of us at a time. Even if they were perfectly turned out, well, we would still find some nit-picky little fault. Of course, everyone loved it!

Roll-call was followed by a snack lunch, then usually, we'd hold a workshop or discussion group in the afternoon. It would be anything we wanted to learn about or to talk about. So, if a particular Mistress wanted to learn and practice caning, then we would have a caning workshop; or single-tail workshop, where they would practice using the single-tail whip; or a foot worship workshop. Anything at all.

The discussion groups were very important and thoroughly enjoyed. In this lifestyle/hobby people often don't get to talk face to face to each other; it can be quite isolating for some, and at these breaks we talked about all sorts. A very popular and interesting group was always when people talked about how they got into this weird, wonderful and often extreme lifestyle and, when it's done correctly and you meet the right people, how therapeutic it can be and how it can fill a void in your life.

If a Mistress was new to the area and she wanted a chauffeur-driven trip out, then she would have a chauffeur-driven trip out by our chauffeur, complete with his cap and his Mercedes, in which he would ferry her all over the County. There could be shopping trips, afternoon tea ... whatever they wanted to do; any sights they wanted to visit, anything like that. It was great fun.

At dinner, place-cards displaying the names of each Mistress determined the seating plan, and each were presented with an exquisite printed menu to select from. It was all quality and very high class.

The evening meal was a three-course meal decided by me, but cooked by the subs; all under my supervision, of course. The subs would make fresh home-made bread to accompany dinner, then we'd have a starter like paté on toast, prawn cocktail, or soup; main course would be some sort of hotpot, or chicken-in-a-sauce; and dessert was either Eton Mess, Pavlova or a trifle, something along those lines. A cheeseboard selection followed by coffee and mints would be served to finish off with.

All the Mistresses would be served by all the subs, and each had their allotted tasks: serving dishes; clearing the table; doing the washing up; topping up water glasses; while we had the TV maids topping up the wine. It was a glorious evening. Fantastic.

I remember one time when one of the TV maids thought they saw someone they knew. I saw her looking, and then start to say, "Haven't I seen you where I work ... ?"

"Stop it!" I said, quietly seething through clenched teeth, "This is not appropriate!" It was okay for them; they were unrecognisable. She stopped mid-sentence but didn't get invited back again.

She'd lost her chance. Incorrect protocol will *not* be tolerated! Discretion is paramount.

Evenings would be filled with fun and games. Some evenings we'd play and have fun with charades, generally involving humiliating some of the subs; general games with plenty of chit-chat. It was a real female domination evening.

Sometimes the subs performed a pantomime, which was fantastic! The Mistresses would laugh 'til they cried. *Mistress R* from Birmingham, a very well-known and respected Mistress and a wonderful lady – I remember seeing her once in her Mistress life, so severe and so strict – she always used to enjoy the pantomimes. Well, watching this particular pantomime, she was curled up laughing so much that tears ran down her face! She was so relaxed and at ease enjoying the night's entertainment. We all did. It was such fun!

Throughout the event there was a plentiful, diverse supply of activities for the Mistresses to indulge in, and indulge they did! They could go for a sauna if they wanted; or a massage; or their nails painted; anything they wanted, they got. They could even have champagne in the hot tub. It was fantastic! Everything available was listed on the *'Welcome Itinerary Menu'* for their pleasure and choosing, catering to their every whim.

The Weekend Break was so popular we ran it a couple of times a year for a good few years running; a most enjoyable weekend break experience.

We also held *'slave training'* camps. Those slaves had to work *really* hard. This time we were catering for submissives and slaves who were interested in service-type roles. They were trained to exceptional standards, like a super butler. They had to sit written and practical exams on how to peel a grape and serve it as artistically as possible, then we'd hold a small, fun competition for the best grape served. That sort of thing.

The slaves were also instructed to supply seven different names to call their Mistress, all respectful, of course; lots of little things like that. They were marked and graded accordingly, and we held competitions to see who was the best slave of the day.

These are real-life roleplay games, strictly for adults. These weekends filled a gap in people's busy lives; it helped them de-stress, unwind and live their fantasies. They were in a bubble, away from prying eyes and able to be whatever they wanted to be. It can be very powerful for some.

We also provided 'maid training' camps for TV crossdressers, who wanted to learn more about serving, dressing-up, walking in high heels, and deportment. It was a glorious weekend for those people who wanted to live the lifestyle, twenty-four hours a day, for two or three days.

They got to meet other like-minded people because, in this world, it's quite isolating. It's not the sort of thing you can talk to anyone about. There are quite a few different fetish/kink websites out there, but you very rarely get to meet people, especially if you're quite a private person. And at this event, because it was run by myself, who is trusted and respected on the scene, people realised that discretion and privacy were assured.

That was the most important thing. People came and they were free for seventy-two hours or however long they stayed. We were in a protected 'bubble' away from the stresses and strains of everyday life. It was almost like being hypnotised and at the end, just before you leave, someone clicks their fingers and says, "and back," then whoosh, back to reality.

They were able to relax, do what they enjoyed; quality time for them. Even if it was getting whipped, caned, or grovelling around under their Mistresses' feet, they could freely and openly be themselves, living out their own fantasies or needs without repercussion or judgement.

On occasion at these events, we'd have afternoons where we'd just sit around. Mistresses would inter-mingle with each other, taking their submissives with them and everyone would just go and chat to each other, exchanging their stories of how they got into the lifestyle, their struggles; real heart-to-heart discussions on how they managed to maintain their alternative passions, all sorts of things.

That was very interesting to the other subs because you just don't get to hear that sort of level of intimacy. It was unheard of, people talking so unguardedly. It filled a massive void in those people's lives.

The age group went right across the board. Some were retired, some had professional jobs, some of them were still quite young. Such a variety of different people, but crucially, the important thing was that there was never any judgement. This meant that they could all be open and honest with each other, including themselves. Those were wonderful times. Heady days!

One eventful highlight of fun that happened *at every single 'Mistress Break',* was that one of the Mistresses would always say enthusiastically, once they had donned their finery and looked tremendous, "Come on ladies, let's go and visit the local Working Men's Club." It was just down the road, within walking distance. *Please God no!* I used to whisper a silent prayer under my breath every time I heard it suggested. And *every time* I worried that one of them would actually do it! It never did happen, of course, but the fun they got from seeing their subs panicked faces was a picture! It panicked me as well, though I never showed it.

Another incident I remember that happened at one of these *Mistress Breaks.* Earlier in the book, I mentioned Bill, the maintenance man, caretaker/cleaner of the hotel. He was very intrigued by the whole thing, and quite nosy. He often tried to sneak a peek at what was going on, whenever he could find the opportunity.

Well, late Sunday afternoons, there used to be a nudist group that came to the hotel, and sometimes our Mistresses or submissives would arrive just before the nudist group had finished to check-in to their rooms.

Some of them had driven three, four or five hours. Once some of the guests came from as far away as Land's End in their Land Rover! What a trip that must have been! We never turned anybody away if they arrived early, even if it meant they had to walk through the nudist group! Everyone was welcome.

One evening, after the nudist group had gone, Bill thought he had found such an opportunity. By deliberately staying late under the pretext of washing everybody's towels, then hanging them up to dry on the radiators all over the hotel, he had a valid reason for being there by busying himself, going around hanging up all the towels.

By the time he'd finished, the Mistresses were downstairs by the bar, all glammed up to the nines in their leather and lace corsets, boots and hats; fully dressed up, looking absolutely amazing. Although we'd asked Bill not to go in the bar, Bill 'forgot', accidentally on purpose yet again, and wandered into the bar. Immediately Steve was on his case.

"Bill! You can't come into the bar! We told you!"

"Oh, it's alright Steve, I don't mind," came his cheeky retort.

"We know you don't mind Bill. But we mind!" – a little ditty I thought quite funny at the time.

Chapter Twenty-Two

The Final Chapter

Over the years I had established a good business as a Dominatrix and alongside it came the lifestyle I enjoyed tremendously; that is, doing what people found very valuable in order to help balance their lives. That included me balancing my life as well.

I had travelled the UK and the USA visiting places I had only ever dreamed of; I had made myself a base in the UK, hired facilities within a Swingers Club and had kitted the dungeon out to be perfect for my needs; I'd had furniture built and more equipment made.

I had really pushed the boundaries in this alternative and unusual lifestyle. The court events were unique and have since been replicated by others. I had facilitated two- and three-night breaks with a leaning to the activities people loved, and established training events for both maids and slaves. I also organised workshops for all sorts of things, like caning, spanking, flogging, the list goes on ... I felt it crucial that people could learn how to handle equipment, and people, properly. After all, this sport is dangerous! But you can still be safe. The SSC mantra comes to mind again: *Safe, Sane, Consensual.* Three words that mean so much to me.

I had indulged people's fantasies; held court scenarios and kidnaps. I had set up online forums for specialist interests and had even made a very tongue-in-cheek newsletter for my followers! Every Christmas I arranged a photoshoot and made, printed, and sent out personalised Christmas cards from me as a means for them to remember me by, as I did them.

I had even started establishing club events. My first ever event was the *'T Birds Club'*, and it still runs today. One of my then clients had said he was desperate to be around other TV/CDs, and why didn't I run a club? So, I did. The club quickly established itself. There weren't many places then where cross-dressers could freely don their make up, outfits, stockings and heels, then chat and flirt with others who had the same fantasy!

For some this was more than just a fantasy. Some people were exploring their own gender identity and working their way down a long and often lonely road. For others, this was a haven of normality; no hassle, just fun, friendly, and welcoming people in a bubble that kept out the negativity they felt in every day-to-day life. This process of examining and going through your life, disrupting everything, can be a long, long journey, and a solitary one. So, for a few people, this club is a godsend and a lifeline!

It also provided an outlet for their 'admirers', as we called them. Believe me, there are many admirers. It may not be something they shout from the rooftops, but there is always a steady stream of admirers; mainly male, but often females, and sometimes couples as well.

By this time, I had a modest income; not rich financially by any means, but rich in experiences of people and places, and the freedom to control my own destiny. This is a very liberating thing for a lady of my age. My confidence in myself had grown and the depth of my integrity and principles had been honed and developed. I could do whatever I wanted and whatever I decided. That is very powerful; very powerful indeed. Wonderful.

Then something shattered that peace!

The owner of the Swingers' Club decided he wanted out and asked me if I wanted to buy the place. Goodness me! Just as life was good and settled, this curveball landed on my lap!

To buy! That took one hell of a nerve, and what a business risk! And I wasn't a swinger! I was a free spirit, a maverick, one that revelled in my anonymity – and even notoriety – and always under the radar! I thought deep and hard. *Operating under the radar in this secret life I lead is one thing, this is the total opposite end of the spectrum; but to refuse this offer would mean someone else would take over and I'd have no security. I've spent a small fortune building my purpose-built dungeon and could risk losing it all!*

All sorts of anxious questions were running through my head! *What if I didn't buy it? The new owners may not agree to the same terms I already have. We may not get on. They may kick me out and use it for themselves …* What a dilemma!

I completed a thorough risk analysis of the possible options, their benefits, associated risks, threats, and opportunities. In the end, buying the place won out – narrowly! But, in my eyes, it was my best option. Interestingly, my faithful submissive Andrew was dead-set against me taking it on. He was a bit of a dinosaur really, but it didn't stop him putting everything into helping me achieve my dream. Such was his dedication and loyalty.

I managed to raise the money with the help of some very supportive and loyal 'lifestyle' friends, took on debt, and the purchase was finalised. I had bought the leasehold of the premises and the business that went with it! How exciting! How scary! How daunting! And how my boundaries were going to be pushed! Though little did I know at the time, the club owner decided to make an announcement on the Saturday night. It was Halloween!

The swingers are a fairly small community and they had got wind that the club was for sale. They were itching to know who was going to take it over. There was so much speculation, but no-one seemed to have any idea. Over one hundred people came to the club that night to see the new owner. Being the sort of people they are, I was made to feel very welcome. They cheered and clapped when the announcement was made on the dance floor. I felt humbled to be welcomed with such open arms.

However, a swift baptism of fire ensued.

The council turned up on the Monday to inspect the premises. The previous owner had assured me that, in the legal documentation, all legalities were covered, but hadn't left any paperwork. Very strange. I should have heard the alarm bells ringing even then, but being new to all this, well, I just hadn't realised.

Rubbish! He hadn't done anything by the book! I had to spend thousands more re-wiring and getting the fire system sorted out. He was dishonest and I had trusted him; a hard lesson. To take him to court would have cost more money that I didn't have. A bitter pill to swallow.

The Freehold Owner of the building was really, really angry that the previous lessee had made money out of her building by selling the business on without giving her a cut. She took it out on me! And still, to this day, she is being as difficult as she can.

It's been interesting to see that for every idea I had, whether it be wild or simply plain crazy, there was always someone there to help me achieve my dreams, my fantasies, my travels, and all the stages in between. They say that some people come into your life for a season, some come for a reason, and some come for life. I have met plenty of the former people in this business, but few that have come into my life, for life.

That is until I met Bob. He was introduced to me by the original club owner; Bob ran the dungeon parties. Well, we hit it off straight away and we have never looked back. He has helped me build the dungeon and make equipment, took part in the photo-shoots and helped with the *Weekend Breaks*. He is a qualified masseur and carpenter and I have made use of those skills so many times for so many years – and I still do!

But one skill he has which is quite extraordinary is that he is very sensitive to people's feelings. He is always very welcoming to people who may be shy, scared or needing reassurance. He always, and I mean *always*, puts people's enjoyment first and always says the right thing at the right time, putting people at ease.

I have seen him saddled and ridden like a pony; a rope tied to his nether regions and made to run around after the Mistresses; he was even caned and photographed for my Christmas Cards despite caning not being his 'thing'. A good sport? An extraordinary man? The best friend I could ever have? All of those and more. It's difficult to explain how this man has made my world a better place. He has listened to me moan, and moan, and then moan some more; he has laughed with me; he has been there to give me that little nudge, or a few kind and wise words when times have been hard. Money cannot buy a man like Bob, and neither can words describe what he has done. He's one in a million!

He also helped me financially to buy the venue, but more than that, his support has never wavered, even when I forgot his birthday one Halloween night! I had made a big announcement to celebrate the Club's Anniversary of me 'behind the wheel', not realising it was also Bob's birthday on the same day. He came bounding up from the dungeon, thinking I was announcing his birthday, only to be sorely disappointed. I had forgotten! That was one of the saddest mistakes I have ever made, and will not make again. In this weird and wonderful lifestyle, friends like Bob are more valuable than diamonds!

Many people have had an influence on me. Many people helped me along the way, and there were a few that really had a very big and positive impact on me, some of which have already been mentioned earlier in the book. Although at times when I am eager or passionate about things, I do have a tendency to interrupt, I also listen, go away and then think. I am a slow burner in that respect.

And yes, life was good. I run a successful Club and I had honed my skills as a Mistress. I was one of the best. And in this game the other Mistresses that are the best, are the incredible women I encountered. We all put a slightly different spin on our art, on our skill. Some made video clips for online; some were the most beautiful women dressed in leather or latex ... fantasy women they were. And then there was little old round and fat me!

My reputation was not for my looks or my dress code, but for what I *did*! And that meant more to me than looks or money; much, much more! I fiercely honour and protect that reputation by doing what I say I will; being straight with people, despite it sometimes being hard to take; and by my endeavours to keep people safe in their own choices, however wild they may be.

We all had our place. This lifestyle is so diverse. I never once found myself being intimidated by any of the other Mistresses; they had their skills and attributes and I had mine. And every

Mistress behaved and treated their fellow conspirators with the utmost respect. After all, it is all part of this lifestyle.

I found out much, much later, that a married couple, central to the Swingers Club when I first took the Club over, had said they would give me three months before I would give up; that I wouldn't be able to 'cut the mustard.'

"She's not a swinger! She'll never be able to run this place!"

And of course, when I found this out, well, the gauntlet was down – and the rest speaks for itself!

So here I stand, at the end of one era and straight into another! Running that merry-go-round that must never stop, the club that is *Clubf*. But that's a whole new never-ending story! Fun, laughter, tears, exhaustion. Until COVID came, that is ...

A Note from the Ghostwriter

I was first introduced to the real world of BDSM through the Swingers Club owned by Madam Rattan which I'd joined as a swinger. Having worked abroad in the sex industry and on the striptease circuit for seven years, a sex club with dancing was music to my ears!

Since being back in 'civvy street', however, I had found it really difficult to 'fit in' anywhere outside of my two greatest passions, sex and dancing; I had always felt like a square peg in a round hole. I had experienced so much that is beyond the everyday.

I love being in Madam Rattan's Club. It feels like home. It was strange having sex with many people and not getting paid, but I didn't care. It was a completely different vibe, worlds away from my professional experiences, yet I felt I was back in familiar territory. It's a great club, very friendly, I was made to feel very welcome and ... it has a dungeon!

I used to visit the dungeon for massage and light flogging. I discovered I liked it, though I didn't really know anything about the scene and how to get involved. Bob was my masseur and he remembered me from my early go-go dancing days in the local clubs and bars, before I'd travelled abroad. It was wonderful! It was Bob who answered my burning questions about the lifestyle and the club's involvement in the scene.

I've always had submissive tendencies and a submissive nature. I knew that. But Bob's stories about the lifestyle, the dungeon in the club, together with my desire to make it into a reality, really gave me the impetus to do something about it.

New Beginnings ...

It was visiting a family friend, a couple down south, that became my defining moment. They used to have a BDSM relationship/dynamic with a young submissive called Shannon who, at the time, had a Mistress, and were planning to attend a munch when I was there. Shannon and my friend Denise were happy to tell me what it was all about and told me about FetLife. Shannon suggested I set up a profile before the munch. It made sense to me because it showed I was serious and not just being 'curious'.

I set up my profile and went to the munch – and it was wonderful. The people were so open and friendly, and so diverse; all ages. One woman was given coloured rope as a gift. How lovely. I just sat back quietly, watched, and listened. I was intrigued. I absorbed it all like a sponge. I wanted to find out more.

Back home I developed my profile and went to a few munches by myself in my local area to meet people. I started to recognise people. Everywhere I went, I was always made to feel welcome. Gradually I was offered friend requests on FetLife, so I could follow threads of discussion and involve myself more if I wanted.

One day there was a request for a voluntary librarian advertised in one of my local groups. *Yes! That's for me!* I thought. *I love books! Especially when they're about kink and sex! Perfect! I might even get the chance to read some and learn more about BDSM!* I was excited. I applied. I was invited to the premises to 'have a chat' ...

... And the premises were Madam Rattan's club! I officially got to meet Madam Rattan!

"Good afternoon, Madam Rattan, pleased to meet you. I am Miss-Appropriate!" I said as we shook hands. We had met before, but never in relation to the BDSM side of things. From that moment on, I became part of the BDSM scene. I also changed my profile name to something more suitably submissive once I learned protocol.

My acceptance of being a submissive has given me such ease and great relief! It has dramatically turned my life around for the better. I can be myself; I am a submissive and I'm proud of it. It gives me deep joy and satisfaction. That is where I belong. This is who I am.

Being a submissive, to me, represents freedom from suppressed emotions and repressed authenticity. It allows me the freedom to be me. My personal choice without retribution, my balance. The freedom to freely express my emotion of joy and bliss; that self-expressive expansion and growth that is Self.

The Next Step ...

And now I have this fantastic opportunity to be ghostwriter for Madam Rattan's book, which is indeed a privilege and an honour. This has also created another defining moment for me, and right now, it's literally, staring me right in the face! The research gathered from Madam Rattan has provided me with an insight of where I *do* want to go from here.

Whilst reading through the memorabilia Madam Rattan provided for research material for her book, some of it 'hit a nerve'. I felt I had been punched in the stomach; I felt it to my very core. And I couldn't ignore it. It was the information leaflet of the *'KinkCon Workshop'* held by Madam Rattan that knocked me for six. The demonstrations, the workshops, the lectures ... they all fascinated me. *I want to be there! I want to be a part of it!*

I know I am an exhibitionist, which I've experienced through my dancing and sex. I like to perform, and I like to entertain. I know I am a submissive; It's innate. It's undeniable. It's in the very core of me and now I feel I want to express and experience the *'more'*.

The memorabilia made me realise how strong my desire to become more of a submissive really is; to live the life I have chosen, that is indelibly etched into the very fabric of my being; the shadow of my past interwoven from my life experiences to date, now in plain sight. I want more of the lifestyle. I want to serve more. I want to *be* more. I want to experience the *more*!

Now I want to delve further and deeper into this lifestyle. I would like to experience wax play and rope play; to explore confinement; objectification; role-play and predicament bondage. But pain! Can I take pain? Real punishment? I want to explore ... I want to know ...

And I'm excited ...

And Other Subs' Stories ...

A Slave's Memoirs – Sub 2

Sklavos, a slave who features in Madam Rattan's memoirs in this book, has kindly written and submitted his own memoirs of specific memorable events he experienced during his time with Madam Rattan; kindly reproduced as below ...

Sklavos met Madam Rattan through *'collarme'* in 2006. Madam Rattan required a London slave to serve Her when visiting, approximately once a month, for her caning sessions. A loan agreement, the details of which sklavos was never apprised of, was reached between Madam Rattan and sklavos' Owner. sklavos served Madam Rattan for over a year and had many wonderful adventures in Her service, the most of which are described below.

1. Madam Rattan became part of the London judicial punishment scene and would visit London to cane clients and visit caning events. In one such trip, She came to London with a friend, who was a budding FemDom. sklavos was ordered to pick Them up at Euston and drive Them to Their hotel in Canary Wharf. Madam Rattan always stayed in a Hilton hotel. Meeting Them outside the station, parking illegally, opening doors for the Mistresses and getting Their luggage and canes in the boot of his sports car was always a challenge, but also exciting. During the drive to the hotel, Madam Rattan would inform sklavos of Her schedule and any particular arrangements She required of sklavos.

    At the hotel, sklavos would carry the multiple suitcases and canes to Their rooms and unpack Their suitcases while They enjoyed a drink, and then assist Them in preparing for Their first session. sklavos would drive Them to the dungeon, make the final preparations, and would be locked in a small room or closet during the session(s). When the session(s) would end, sklavos would clean up, ensuring that the dungeon was sparkling clean, and take Madam Rattan and Her Domme friend to dinner, which Madam Rattan always enjoyed, wanting to try different cuisines, then back to the hotel to carry everything up to the room.

2. During another trip to London, Madam Rattan came by Herself and was staying at the Hilton in Kensington. At Her room, sklavos emptied Madam's suitcase and was then ordered to prepare the bath for Madam. Madam liked Her bath to be steaming hot. Following Her bath, sklavos was instructed to give Madam a relaxing massage and was ordered to worship Her feet while She napped prior to Her evening caning sessions. This time the dungeon was at Tottenham Court – a lovely two room dungeon.

   The memorable event for sklavos was that Madam loaned him to the dungeon Owner to clean Her flat, which was above the dungeon. While Madam Rattan delivered Her judicial punishment to Her clients, sklavos was vacuuming, dusting, and cleaning the kitchen while the dungeon Owner watched TV. The evening concluded with a Moroccan dinner at Bayswater. Back at the hotel, sklavos would assist Madam getting ready for bed and was ordered to worship Her feet until She fell asleep. sklavos would sleep on the floor next to Her bed and was provided with a pillow but no blanket, as this was Madam's preference.

3. Another memorable event was being ordered to drive to Madam's house for a weekend of service. sklavos left London early and arrived at Madam's house around 10.00am. After greeting Madam by kneeling and kissing Her feet, sklavos was directed to Her backyard where he was ordered to complete

the garden work alongside Madam's primary slave. This was hard work that lasted several hours – Madam would inspect from inside Her warm kitchen.

The evening activities involved preparing dinner for Madam and her Domme friend. Madam's slave and sklavos cooked an English-Greek dinner combination, which we served to Madam and Her guest. Our attire was being nude but required a bow tie. We served dinner and were then ordered to worship Their feet under the dining table while the Ladies ate. Madam had us eat the leftovers from plates on the floor while the Ladies watched us and commented. Following dinner, we provided foot massages to Madam and Her friend while They relaxed and chatted. Madam's main slave was dismissed for the night and sklavos assisted Madam in getting ready for bed, licked Her feet until She fell asleep, and slept on the floor naked, wearing a collar, with a pillow but not a blanket.

4. Perhaps the most memorable adventure was a weekend Christmas dinner at the Femdom Society UK. Madam Rattan had become a member – She actually did a caning video with the Femdom Society – and was invited to the exclusive event with Her slaves. Madam drove to the cottage with sklavos, meeting Her main slave on the way there. Madam had Her slaves bring Santa hats, bow ties, champagne, and chocolate for the Ladies.

On arrival, Madam socialised with the Ladies while sklavos and Her main slave were sent to Her room to unpack. Madam came to the room later – they greeted Her naked on their knees, kissing Her feet. She instructed both of them to prepare Her for dinner, which included a bath, massage, and dressing Her in Her gown. The slaves were all nude, wearing their bow ties or collars, and they had their Santa hats on. In all, there were approximately 12 Ladies in attendance and between 12–15 slaves and sissy maids. Dinner was prepared by the slave chef and was served to the Ladies by the maids – the slaves were all ordered to stay in the kitchen.

Following dinner, the Ladies gathered in the grand salon where several activities involving the slaves were to take place. The slaves would dance, sing, and do other humiliating things to amuse the Ladies. All the Ladies were dressed in gowns and enjoyed a drink while the slaves amused Them. sklavos and Madam's main slave had practiced a dancing/singing routine to amuse the Ladies, which was received well by Them, since the follow-up whipping by Madam Rattan was rather mild. We spent the rest of the evening at Madam's feet being Her footstool and holding Her drink.

Back at Her room, we assisted Madam to bed, each slave worshipped one foot until She fell asleep, and then slept at either side of Her bed naked, wearing only our bow ties, with a pillow but no blanket, as per Madam's custom.

EIN HERZ FÜR AUTOREN A HEART FOR AUTHORS À L'ÉCOUTE DES AUTEURS MIA ΚΑΡΔΙΑ ΓΙΑ ΣΥΓΓΡΑ
HJÄRTA FÖR FÖRFATTARE UN CORAZÓN POR LOS AUTORES YAZARLARIMIZA GÖNÜL VERELIM SZÍV
CUORE PER AUTORI ET HJERTE FOR FORFATTERE EEN HART VOOR SCHRIJVERS TEMOS OS AUTOR
HERZÖINKÉRT SERCE DLA AUTORÓW EIN HERZ FÜR AUTOREN A HEART FOR AUTHORS À L'ÉCOUT
RAÇÃO ΜΙΑ ΚΑΡΔΙΑ ΓΙΑ ΣΥΓΓΡΑΦΕΙΣ UN CUORE PER AUTORI ET HJERTE FOR FORFATTERE EEN H.
ARLARIMIZA GÖ ERE ZÖINKÉRT SERCE DLA AUTORÓW EIN HERZ FÜR
OR SCHRIJVERS S O   AÇÃO ВСЕЙ ДУШОЙ К АВТОРАМ ETT HJÄRTA FÖR

The author

Now approaching retirement, Madam Rattan
has lived a full & colourful life, filled with love,
laughter & family. Career choices have enabled
travel to some far flung & exotic locations for both
business & pleasure providing Madam Rattan
with a life experience the like of which most of us
cannot imagine. It gives her a unique perspective
of some of the darker areas of the human
experience.